STUDENT UNIT

A2 Chemistry
UNIT 2849

OCR

Salters

Module 2849: Chemistry of Materials

Frank Harriss

A2 Chemistry

To Maggi

Thanks to Gwen Pilling for her help with the Content Guidance section of this guide

Philip Allan Updates
Market Place
Deddington
Oxfordshire
OX15 0SE

tel: 01869 338652
fax: 01869 337590
e-mail: sales@philipallan.co.uk
www.philipallan.co.uk

© Philip Allan Updates 2004

ISBN 1 84489 006 6

All rights reserved; no part of this publication may be reproduced, stored in a retrieval system, or transmitted, in any form or by any means, electronic, mechanical, photocopying, recording or otherwise without either the prior written permission of Philip Allan Updates or a licence permitting restricted copying in the United Kingdom issued by the Copyright Licensing Agency Ltd, 90 Tottenham Court Road, London W1P 9HE.

This Guide has been written specifically to support students preparing for the OCR Salters A2 Chemistry Unit 2849 examination. The content has been neither approved nor endorsed by OCR or Salters and remains the sole responsibility of the author.

Printed by Information Press, Eynsham, Oxford

OCR *(Salters)* Unit 2849

A2 Chemistry

Contents

Introduction

About this guide 4
How to use this guide 4
Revision and examination technique 5

■ ■ ■

Content Guidance

About this section 12
Organic chemistry 13
Condensation polymers 20
Proteins 26
Genes and protein synthesis 31
Equilibrium 34
Reaction rates 36
Transition metals 39
Steel 43
Redox 44
Analytical methods 50

■ ■ ■

Questions and Answers

About this section 56
Q1 Steel for a surgeon 57
Q2 The enzyme urease 66
Q3 A biodegradable plastic 74
Q4 Preventing steel boats from rusting 82
Q5 Liniment 85

Introduction

About this guide

This guide is designed to help you prepare for the first Salters A2 Chemistry unit test, which examines the content of **Module 2849: Chemistry of Materials**. This module is divided into four sections: **What's in a medicine?**, **Designer polymers**, **Engineering proteins** and **The steel story**.

The aim of this guide is to provide you with a clear understanding of the requirements of the unit and to advise you on how best to meet those requirements.

The book is divided into the following sections:
- This **Introduction**, which outlines revision and examination technique, showing you how to prepare for the unit test.
- **Content Guidance**, which provides a summary of all the 'chemical ideas' in Module 2849, together with important revision ideas from previous modules.
- **Questions and Answers**, in which you will find questions in the same style as in the unit test, followed by the answers of two students, one of whom is likely to get an A grade, the other a C/D grade. Examiner's comments follow these answers.

How to use this guide

- Read the section 'Revision and examination technique' in this Introduction.
- Decide on the amount of time you have available for chemistry revision.
- Allocate suitable amounts of time to:
  - each section of the Content Guidance, giving the most time to the areas that seem most unfamiliar
  - the questions in the Questions and Answers section
- Draw up a revision timetable, allocating the time for questions later in your timetable.
- When revising sections of the Content Guidance:
  - read the guidance and look at corresponding sections in your notes and textbooks
  - write your own revision notes
  - try questions from past unit tests and from other sources, such as *Chemical Ideas*.
- When using the Questions and Answers:
  - try to answer the question yourself
  - then look at the students' answers, together with your own, and try to work out the best answer
  - then look at the examiner's comments

OCR *(Salters)* Unit 2849

Revision and examination technique

Do I have to remember material from the AS units?

Yes, but only if the ideas are revisited in the four topics contained in this unit. For example, much of the chemistry in **Designer polymers** and **What's in a medicine?** links back to work covered in **The polymer revolution**. **Engineering proteins** contains material on equilibrium and rates that you first met in **The atmosphere**. **The steel story** has material on redox from **Minerals to elements**.

How do I find what to learn?

Well, we hope this book will be useful to you! Other sources are:
- the specification. This is the definitive one. If it's not in the specification (either for this module or as a point revisited from a previous module), it won't be in the paper! However, the specification is written in 'examiner-speak', so it might not always be absolutely clear what is required. This guide should help you to interpret the module content — every specification point is covered in the Content Guidance section. The specification also guides you to the material you need from previous modules, which is listed at the end of each section as 'links to other teaching modules'.
- the 'Check your notes' activities in the *Activities* pack. These also suggest sources of details not found in the *Chemical Ideas* book. Some of the material is in the *Storylines* book and some in the activity sheets.
- your own and your teacher's notes. Preparation for an exam is not just something you do shortly before you take the paper. It should be an integral part of your daily work in chemistry.
- the 'Concept maps' in the *Teacher's and Technician's Guide* are also helpful, especially when deciding which synoptic material is needed. Ask your teacher for these.

How much of *Storylines* and *Activities* do I need to learn?

Have a look through for yourself, but you will find the details in the 'Check your notes' activity sheets referred to above.

The primary function of the *Storylines* book is to provide a framework and a justification for studying the theory topics. For all four topics in this unit, there are important parts of the theory in *Storylines*.

The activity sheets are provided to teach practical and other skills and to back up the theoretical ideas. However, they also contain some theory that does not occur elsewhere.

General revision tips

Revision is a personal thing
What works for one person does not necessarily work for another. You should by now have some idea about what methods suit you, but here are a few ways to set out your revision notes:
- mind maps — ideas radiate out from a central point and are linked together; some people like to colour these in
- notes with bullet points and headings
- small cards with a limited 'bite-size' amount of material on each

Make a plan
Divide up your material into sections (the Content Guidance section will be helpful here). Then:
- work out how much time you have available before the exam
- allocate each section as much time as you can, bearing in mind which you feel you nearly understand and which are the most difficult
- fit this in with any revision your teacher is going to do — ask him or her for a summary

Write, write, write!
Whatever you do, make sure that your revision is *active*, not just flipping over the pages saying 'yeah, yeah, I know this already'. Write more revision notes, test yourself (or each other), *try questions*.

Test yourself
- Questions in *Chemical Ideas* are useful 'drill exercises' on topics, but are not all like exam questions.
- If you have taken end of unit tests, go through them again and then check your answers against the corrected version or the model answers you may have been given. These are much more like exam questions.
- Past papers are available and they give you a good indication of what you will be facing.
- The Questions and Answers section of this book is designed for this purpose.

Know the enemy — the exam paper

I hope, since you will have prepared properly, you will be able to look on the exam as an opportunity to show what you can do, rather than as a battle! Be aware, however, that you must prepare yourself for an exam just as you would for an important sporting contest — be focused. Work hard right through the 90 minutes and don't dwell on difficulties — put them behind you. Try to emerge feeling worn out but happy that you have done your best, even if you have found it difficult (others will probably feel the same way). Then forget it and don't have a post-mortem.

Every question tells a story
Salters is all about learning chemistry in relevant (i.e. real-life) contexts, so it is right that the exam questions should reflect this. Sometimes the context will come from

OCR (Salters) Unit 2849

Storylines, sometimes it will be a new one. Look carefully at the 'stem' (the introduction at the top of the question). Most of the important facts here will be needed somewhere in the question. Sometimes, small, additional stems are added later on. These are important too.

90 marks in 90 minutes
It is important to pace yourself through the paper so you can tell whether you are ahead of, or behind, the clock. There is a grid on the front of the paper that gives the marks for each question, which will be helpful here. It is best to work through the paper in order, from the beginning to the end, since the first question is intended to be one of the easier ones. There are usually four or five questions.

45/45 knowledge/application of knowledge
This one you may not know about. Of the total, 45 marks test your knowledge and ask about things you will have learned. The other 45 marks are for the application of that knowledge to new situations or through doing calculations. These questions often begin with 'Suggest…' to make it clear that you are not expected to be able to recall the answer. There are approximately the same number of marks on chemical ideas from **Engineering proteins** as there are on chemical ideas from **The steel story**, and fewer on **Designer polymers** and **What's in a medicine?**, which are shorter topics.

Easy and hard parts
The papers are designed so that, ideally, an A-grade candidate will get 80% (72 out of 90) and an E-grade candidate 40% (36 out of 90). The actual mark for each grade varies between papers, depending on the difficulty, and is only decided after all the papers have been marked. Some of the parts are designed with A-grade candidates in mind and so will seem quite demanding. Other parts are designed to allow an E-grade candidate to score 40% and so will seem rather easy. Thus, there are easy, middling and hard parts within each question.

Dealing with different types of question

Short-answer questions
These are the most straightforward, but remember:
- look at the marks available — make one good point per mark.
- look at the number of lines — this gives *some* idea of the length of answer required. Of course, handwriting varies greatly in size, but if you have written two words and there are three lines, you can assume you have not written enough to score full marks!
- don't 'hedge your bets' — if you give two alternative answers, you will not get the marks unless *both* are right. For example, if the answer is 'hydrogen bond' and you write 'hydrogen bond or permanent dipole–permanent dipole force', you will score zero.
- read the question — don't answer a question that you have made up! Examiners do have kind hearts really, and they are genuinely sorry when they have to award zero for an answer containing good chemistry that is not relevant to the question asked. This is a problem with units that are examined twice a year. There are lots

of past papers around, all asking slightly different questions on the same subject-matter. It's all too easy to give the answer to last year's question.

Long-answer questions

In this unit test, about 10% of the marks are for extended answers. The same rules apply about marks, lines and reading the question. In addition:
- think before you write ('put brain into gear before operating hand') — perhaps jot a few points in the margin. Try to make your points logically.
- punch those points — if you have read any mark-schemes you will see that they give examiners advice on the weakest answer that will still just score the mark. Make sure your points are made well and win the mark without requiring a second's hesitation by the examiner.
- try to write clear sentences (though bullet points might be appropriate on some occasions).
- be sure you do not re-state the question, i.e. don't use words or phrases directly from the question as part of your explanation.

'In this question, one mark is available for quality of written communication'

There is one such mark in this unit, awarded for part of one question.

The mark is awarded if:
- the answer is written in sentences
- the answer is logical
- the answer shows a correct understanding of technical terms
- spelling, punctuation and grammar are accurate

So, plan your answer more carefully and write in sentences here. Also, use correct chemical terminology, for example 'molecules' rather than 'particles', where appropriate.

Command words in questions

A lot of care is taken in choosing which of these words to use, so note them carefully:
- 'state', 'write down', 'give' and 'name' require short answers only
- 'describe' requires an accurate account of the main points, but no explanation
- 'explain' requires chemical reasons for the statement given
- 'suggest' means that you are not expected to know the answer but you should be able to work it out from what you do know
- 'giving reason(s)' requires you to explain why you chose to answer as you did (if 'reasons' in the plural is stated, judge the number required from the number of marks)

Avoid vague answers

Sometimes it is clear that the candidate knows quite a lot about the topic but his or her answer is not focused. Avoid these words:
- 'it' (e.g. 'it is bigger') — give the name of the thing you are describing, otherwise it may not be very clear which object in the question is being referred to

OCR (Salters) Unit 2849

- 'harmful' — if you mean 'toxic' or 'poisonous', say so!
- 'environmentally friendly' — say *why* it benefits the environment
- 'expensive' — always justify this word with a reason

Be careful with chemical particles — always think twice whenever you write 'particle', 'atom', 'molecule' or 'ion', and check that you are using the correct term.

If in doubt, write something

Try to avoid leaving any gaps. Have a go at every answer. If you are not sure, write something that seems to be sensible chemistry. As you will see from the Questions and Answers section, some questions have a variety of possible answers — the only answer that definitely scores zero is a blank.

Diagrams

You would be amazed at some of the diagrams examiners have to mark, so please:
- read the question. The answer is not always a reflux condenser! If it is an apparatus you know, then it is relatively straightforward. If you have to design something, look for clues in the question.
- make it clear and neat. Use a pencil and a ruler, and have a soft rubber handy to erase any errors.
- make sure it looks like real apparatus (which never has square corners, for example). Some apparatus drawn in exams would test the skill of the most proficient glass-blower.
- draw a cross-section, so that gases can have a clear path through. Don't carelessly leave any gaps where gases could leak out.
- think of safety. Don't suggest heating an enclosed apparatus, which would explode. If a poisonous gas is given off, show it being released in a fume cupboard.
- always label your diagram, especially if the question tells you to. Important things to label are substances and calibrated vessels (e.g. syringes or measuring cylinders).

Calculations

I'll let you into a secret — if you get the answer to a calculation right, the working does not need to be there (unless you could have guessed the answer). However, it is always very easy to make mistakes, especially under the pressure of exams. So, set out the steps in your calculations clearly. Then you will get most of the marks if you make a slight mistake and the examiner can see what you are doing. Examiners operate a system called 'error carried forward' whereby, once an error has been made, the rest of the calculation scores marks if the method is correct from then on.

At the end of the calculation, there will be a line that reads, for example,

Volume =_____   (2 marks)

Obviously you should write your answer clearly here! When you write down your numerical answer, check:
- **units** — most physical quantities have them (sometimes these appear on the answer line to help you)
- **sign** (remember that oxidation states and ΔH values must be shown as '+' if they are positive)
- **significant figures** — you may be expected to analyse uncertainties more carefully in your practical work, but in exam papers all you have to do is to give the same number of significant figures as the data in the question

Content Guidance

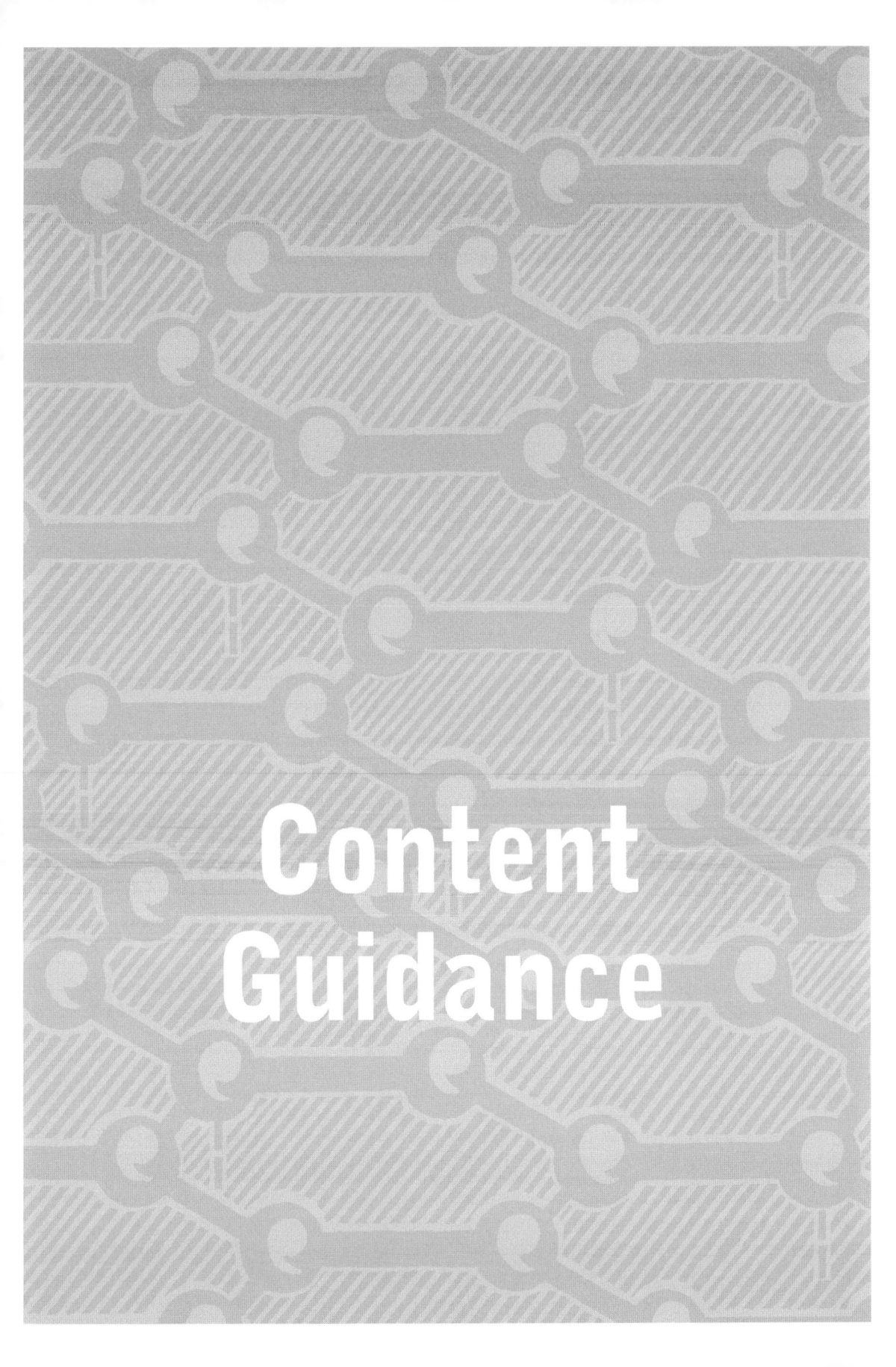

A2 Chemistry

The material in this section summarises the chemical ideas from **Module 2849: Chemistry of Materials**. It is arranged in a logical chemical order, not in the order in which you study it (which is determined by the content of *Storylines*). Revision of AS material is shown in *italics*.

Summary of content

Organic chemistry: functional groups (*part revision*) — amines, amides, carboxylic acids and acyl chlorides; naming acids and esters; phenols; salicylic acid; stereo-isomerism; organic techniques.

Condensation polymers: condensation reactions; hydrolysis; properties of condensation polymers in terms of intermolecular forces and structure; varying the properties; disposal of polymers.

Proteins: amino acids; protein structure; enzymes.

Genes and protein synthesis: DNA; protein synthesis; genetic engineering; making medicines.

Equilibrium: *revision of equilibrium*; the equilibrium constant, K_c; the effect of temperature and pressure on equilibrium.

Reaction rates: the effect of concentration on rate of reaction; *the effect of pressure, temperature, surface area and catalysts on the rate of reaction.*

Transition metals: electronic structure; typical properties — variable oxidation state, complexes, coloured ions, catalytic behaviour.

Steel: types of steel; making steel; recycling.

Redox: *revision of redox*; cells and electrode potentials; use of electrode potentials; rusting.

Analytical methods: colorimetry; manganate(VII) titrations; mass spectrometry, infrared spectroscopy, NMR spectroscopy.

How much of this do I need to learn?

The answer is, virtually all of it. It has been pared down to the absolute essentials. If you need any more detail on any aspect, you should look in your textbooks or notes.

OCR *(Salters)* Unit 2849

Organic chemistry

Functional groups

Type of compound	Functional group	Relevant reactions	Example	Conditions
Alcohol	—OH	Condensation (esterification)	$C_2H_5OH + CH_3COOH \rightarrow CH_3COOC_2H_5 + H_2O$	Reflux; conc. H_2SO_4 catalyst
Phenol	C₆H₅—O—H	Condensation (esterification)	$C_6H_5OH + CH_3COCl \rightarrow CH_3COOC_6H_5 + HCl$	Room temperature; anhydrous
Carboxylic acid	—C(=O)—O—H	Acts as acid	$2CH_3COOH + Na_2CO_3 \rightarrow 2CH_3COO^-Na^+ + CO_2 + H_2O$	Room temperature
		Condensation (esterification)	$C_2H_5OH + CH_3COOH \rightarrow CH_3COOC_2H_5 + H_2O$	Reflux; conc. H_2SO_4 catalyst
Acyl chloride	—C(=O)—Cl	Condensation (acylation)	$CH_3COCl + RNH_2 \rightarrow CH_3CONHR + HCl$ Amide	Room temperature; anhydrous
Primary amine/amino	—NH₂	Acts as base	$RNH_2 + HCl \rightarrow RNH_3^+Cl^-$ Amine salt	Room temperature
		Condensation (forms amides)	$CH_3COCl + RNH_2 \rightarrow CH_3CONHR + HCl$ Amide	Room temperature; anhydrous
Ester	—C(=O)—O—	Hydrolysis	$CH_3COOC_2H_5 + NaOH \rightarrow CH_3COO^-Na^+ + C_2H_5OH$	Reflux; HCl can also be used
Amide	—C(=O)—N(H)—	Hydrolysis	$CH_3CONH_2 + NaOH \rightarrow CH_3COO^-Na^+ + NH_3$	Reflux; HCl can also be used

There is more detail on condensation and hydrolysis on pages 20–26.

Amines

Amines are described as **primary**, **secondary** or **tertiary**. These terms do *not* mean the same as for alcohols. For alcohols, it is the number of alkyl (R) groups on the carbon next to the –OH group which must be counted (one for primary and so on) whereas for amines it is the number of alkyl groups on the nitrogen itself which must be counted.

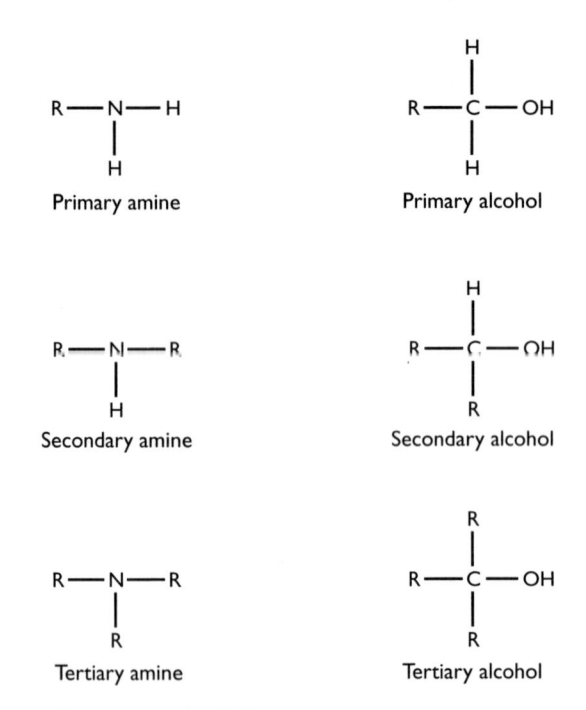

```
    R—N—H              H
       |               |
       H            R—C—OH
                      |
                      H
  Primary amine   Primary alcohol


    R—N—R              H
       |               |
       H            R—C—OH
                      |
                      R
 Secondary amine  Secondary alcohol


    R—N—R              R
       |               |
       R            R—C—OH
                      |
                      R
  Tertiary amine   Tertiary alcohol
```

Simple primary amines are named thus:

```
   H₃C—N—H           C₂H₅—N—H
       |                  |
       H                  H
  is methylamine     is ethylamine
```

Properties of amines
- Amines are basic. They form alkaline solutions in water:
  $RNH_2 + H_2O \longrightarrow RNH_3^+ + OH^-$
- They react with acids to accept a proton:
  $RNH_2 + HCl \longrightarrow RNH_3^+Cl^-$ (an amine salt)
- They undergo **condensation reactions** with acyl chlorides to form amides:

```
  R—N—H + Cl—C—CH₃  →  R—N—C—CH₃ + H—Cl
      |         ||           |  ||
      H         O            H  O
```

This is also known as **acylation**.

Amides

Amides contain the group:

$$-\underset{\underset{H}{|}}{N}-\underset{\underset{O}{\|}}{C}-$$

Primary and secondary amides are defined in a similar way to primary and secondary amines.

Primary amide
(one carbon atom attached to N)

Secondary amide
(two carbon atoms attached to N)

Carboxylic acids and acyl chlorides

Carboxylic acids are met in **What's in a medicine?** They contain the group:

$$-\underset{\underset{O}{\|}}{C}-O-H$$

The proton is relatively easily lost from this group.

Acyl chlorides can be made from carboxylic acids (by a reaction you do not need to remember — it's reaction 6 on the *Data Sheet*).

They contain the group:

$$-\underset{\underset{O}{\|}}{C}-Cl$$

The presence of the C=O makes the C–Cl bond very reactive. Thus, while carboxylic acids have to be heated with alcohols to make esters, acyl chlorides only need to be mixed with alcohols at room temperature.

R—O—H + H—O—C—R' (Conc. H₂SO₄ catalyst, Reflux) → R—O—C—R' + H₂O

Alcohol   Acid   Ester

R—O—H + Cl—C—R' (Mix, Anhydrous conditions*) → R—O—C—R' + H—Cl

Alcohol   Acyl chloride   Ester

*Acyl chlorides react with water

Acyl chlorides also condense with amines when they are mixed at room temperature (see above).

A2 Chemistry

Naming acids and esters

Carboxylic acids

These are named by counting *all* the carbon atoms. For example:

CH_4	methane
C_3H_8	propane
HCOOH	methanoic acid
C_2H_5COOH	propanoic acid

Esters

When naming esters, remember that they are made from an acid reacting with an alcohol. Identify the alcohol group (attached to the O) and name it methyl, ethyl etc. Then identify the acid group (including the C=O) and name this ethanoate, propanoate etc.

Tip Note that the formulae of esters can be written either way round, as these examples show:

Ester	Alcohol (dark area)	Acid (white area)	Name
$CH_3-C(=O)-O-CH_3$	Methanol — thus 'methyl'	Ethanoic acid — thus 'ethanoate'	Methyl ethanoate
$CH_3-CH_2-O-C(=O)-H$	Ethanol — thus 'ethyl'	Methanoic acid — thus 'methanoate'	Ethyl methanoate

Phenols

Phenols have an –OH group attached to a benzene ring.

A benzene ring is written as ⬡. It has six carbon atoms in a flat (planar) ring, each with one hydrogen atom joined to it. Thus, three of the electrons from carbon are used up in forming single bonds, leaving one electron per carbon spare. These electrons are spread over all the carbon atoms, in a process known as **delocalisation**. This is explained in detail in **Colour by design** in Module 2854.

The –OH group in phenol replaces one of the hydrogen atoms, so phenol is C_6H_5OH. The delocalised structure of the benzene ring gives phenol different properties from alcohols:
- they react with neutral iron(III) chloride solution to give a purple colour
- they do not react with acids to form esters; they only react with the more reactive acyl chlorides (see the table on page 13)
- they are weak acids in solution; they come between alcohols (not detectably acidic) and carboxylic acids —

    $C_2H_5OH \longleftarrow H^+ + C_2H_5O^-$ (the reaction does not occur from left to right)
    $C_6H_5OH \rightleftharpoons H^+ + C_6H_5O^-$
    $CH_3COOH \rightleftharpoons H^+ + CH_3COO^-$

OCR *(Salters)* Unit 2849

This is because the anion C₆H₅O⁻ is *stabilised by the spreading of some of the negative charge onto the benzene ring*. For alcohols (e.g. ethanol), C₂H₅O⁻ is not stabilised at all. The CH₃COO⁻ anion is also stabilised by delocalisation (more than C₆H₅O⁻).

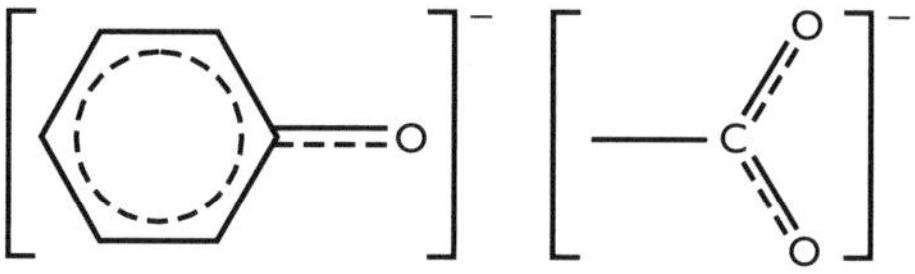

Salicylic acid

Salicylic acid is both a phenol and a carboxylic acid.

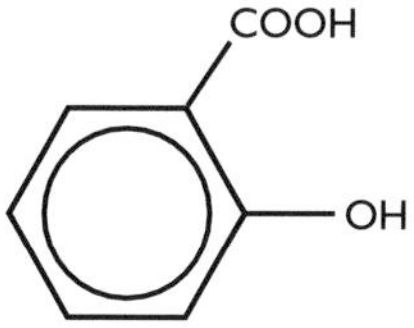

Thus it will:
- form a more acidic solution than phenol (because of the COOH group)
- react with neutral iron(III) chloride to give a pink colour
- react with alcohols to give esters of the –COOH group, for example:

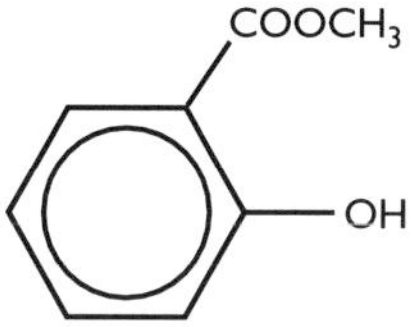

Methyl salicylate — oil of wintergreen

- react with acyl chlorides to give esters of the –OH group, for example:

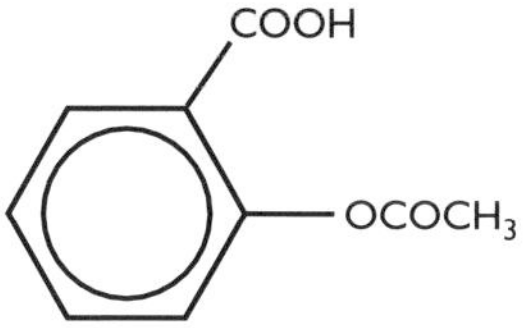

Aspirin

Stereoisomerism

The idea of structural isomers — molecules with the same molecular formula but different structural formulae — was met in **Developing fuels**. Here we look at molecules that have the same structural formula, but differ because of the *arrangement of the atoms in space*.

Geometric isomerism

Cis–trans isomerism was covered in **The polymer revolution**. It can arise when there is a C=C double bond in a molecule. The groups around a C=C bond cannot rotate like those around a C–C bond.

17

A2 Chemistry

- To identify *cis–trans* isomerism, look for a C=C double bond with *two different groups* attached *to each side*.
- To explain *cis–trans* isomerism, refer to the *lack of free rotation* about C=C bonds.

Optical isomerism

You meet optical isomerism in **Engineering proteins**. It occurs when a molecule has a mirror image that is different from the original molecule. The two optical isomers (**enantiomers**) of the amino acid alanine are as follows:

Key
— Bond in plane of paper
▬ Bond coming out of paper
- - - Bond going into paper

Mirror

These molecules are described as **chiral** (from the Greek for hand) because they are related in the same way as right and left hands — they have **non-superimposable** mirror images.

- To identify chiral molecules, look for a carbon atom with *four different groups*.
- To draw chiral molecules, use the style shown in the diagram above — wedge-shaped bonds, lines and dashed lines. Put in a mirror line and draw both the object and its reflection.
- To explain chirality, you should refer to the object and its mirror image as being **non-superimposable**.

Organic techniques

Purifying solids

You meet this in **Designer polymers**.

When an organic solid has been made, it may be purified by **recrystallisation**, which involves the steps in the table below.

Step	Explanation
Dissolve in the *minimum* volume of *hot* solvent (in which the solid is more soluble when the solvent is hot than when it is cold)	The solid being purified must just saturate the hot solvent; impurities — being present in smaller amounts — will not saturate the solvent

OCR*(Salters)* Unit 2849

Step	Explanation
If the solution is cloudy, filter hot	This removes any *insoluble* impurities
Allow the solution to cool and the solid to crystallise — this is the **recrystallisation**; do not let all the solvent evaporate	The required solid is less soluble in cold solvent than in hot solvent, so it will crystallise; impurities remain in solution (unless the solvent evaporates)
Filter off the crystals	The impurities remain in solution
Wash with a little *cold* solvent	This washes off the impurities
Dry (by sucking air through the filter if a volatile solvent has been used)	This removes any remaining solvent

The purity of a solid can be checked by measuring its melting point. An impure solid always melts *below* the expected temperature. Pure substances melt *sharply*, while impure ones melt over a *range of temperatures*.

Thin-layer chromatography
You meet this topic in **What's in a medicine?**
- Spots of unknown and known substances are applied to a base line on a thin-layer plate.
- The plate is placed in a *solvent* (so the spots are above the level of the solvent), in a beaker.
- The beaker is covered.
- The solvent rises up the plate. Its final level is marked.
- The plate is taken out, dried and treated with a locating agent (often UV light or iodine vapour) so the spots show up.
- Spots of the same substance rise to the same characteristic height.
- R_f value = $\dfrac{\text{distance moved by spot}}{\text{distance moved by solvent front}}$

Paper chromatography is similar, except that paper is used in place of a thin-layer chromatography plate (see page 28).

Tip Always draw a diagram if asked to 'describe' chromatography; then describe it in words.

Heating under reflux
This technique is often used in organic chemistry. It involves mounting a water-cooled condenser vertically above a flask. Its purposes are:
- to avoid the loss of vapours (many organic compounds are volatile liquids)
- to avoid fires (many organic compounds are flammable)

Tip You are often asked to draw a diagram of a reflux apparatus.

Note the following:
- Label the heat source and the mixture you are heating.
- Make it apparent that there is a clear path through the apparatus and *do not stopper the top!*

- Show the water connections correctly. Water goes in at the lower connection so that it fills the apparatus, rather than rushing through it.
- Do not (carelessly) leave any gaps through which vapour could escape. (Thus, do not try to represent 'Quickfit' apparatus.)

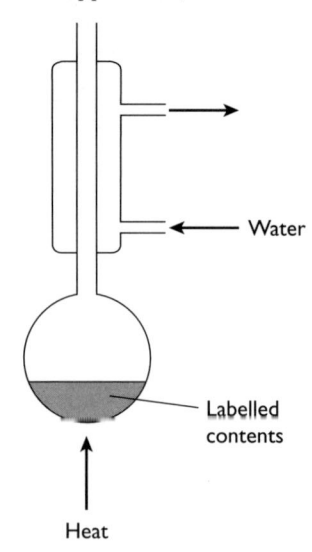

Condensation polymers

You meet this topic in **Designer polymers**.

Condensation reactions

A **condensation** reaction is defined as one in which two molecules join together to make a larger molecule, with the elimination of a small molecule (usually water). **Polymerisation** occurs when many small molecules (**monomers**) join to form a large molecule — the **polymer**. For condensation polymerisation to occur, the monomers must have two reactive groups that can form a polymer chain by condensation reactions.

Note that in addition polymerisation, the monomer has the same empirical (ratio) formula as the polymer, whereas this is not the case for condensation polymers, because a small molecule (e.g. water) is lost.

The two reactions you need to know are **esterification** and **amide formation**. Examples are shown in the table on page 13.

Polyesters

This is how a *di*carboxylic acid and a *di*ol react to form a *poly*ester, the reaction continuing at either end of the chain:

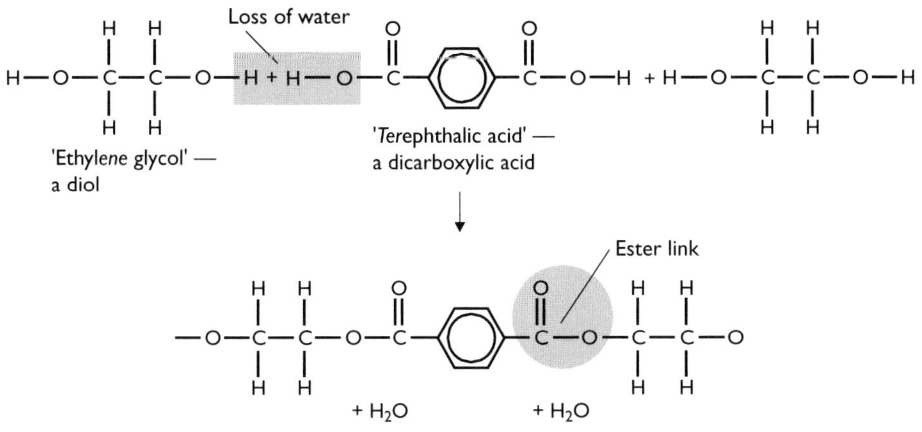

OCR (Salters) Unit 2849

[Diagram showing the reaction of ethylene glycol (a diol) with terephthalic acid (a dicarboxylic acid), with loss of water, forming a polyester ('terylene') containing ester links, + H₂O]

'Ethylene glycol' — a diol

'Terephthalic acid' — a dicarboxylic acid

Polyester ('terylene')

You do not need to know the old names shown in quote marks — they just illustrate how the name 'terylene' came about.

Terylene was designed on purpose; not discovered by accident. The repeat unit is shown below:

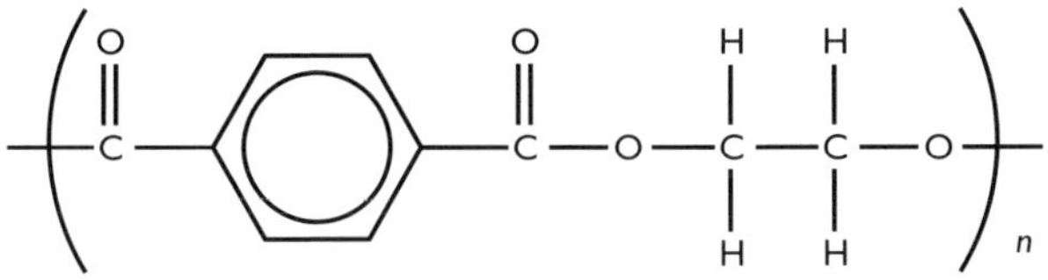

[Structural diagram of the terylene repeat unit, shown with subscript n]

Polyamides

Here, a diamine and a dicarboxylic acid react to form a polyamide, called **nylon**. The reaction can continue at either end of the chain.

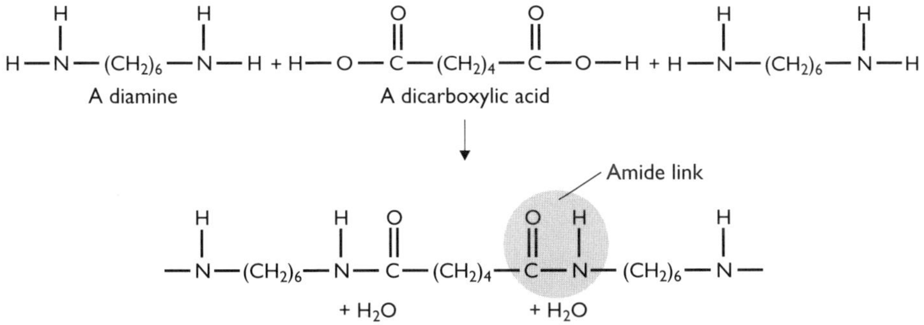

[Diagram showing reaction of a diamine H–N(H)–(CH₂)₆–N(H)–H with a dicarboxylic acid HOOC–(CH₂)₄–COOH forming nylon, a polyamide, with amide links and + H₂O]

A diamine

A dicarboxylic acid

Amide link

Nylon, a polyamide

A scientist called Carothers designed nylon. He modelled the condensing units on the amino acids in proteins and the C–C bonds on addition polymers such as poly(ethene).

The repeat unit is:

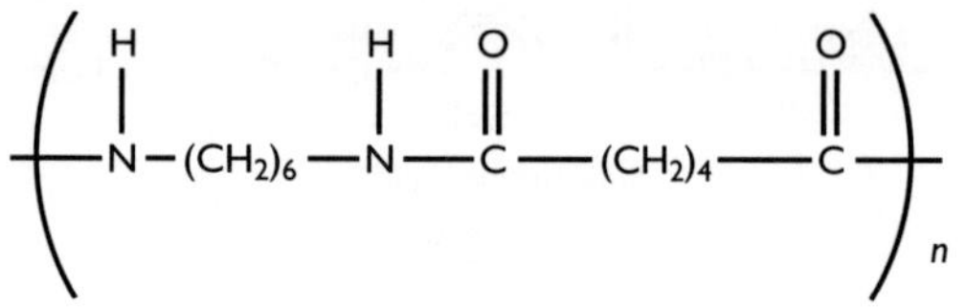

$$\left(-N(H)-(CH_2)_6-N(H)-C(=O)-(CH_2)_4-C(=O)- \right)_n$$

The amino acid shown below has both the amine group and the acid group, so it would polymerise on its own (under the right conditions) to form a slightly different nylon.

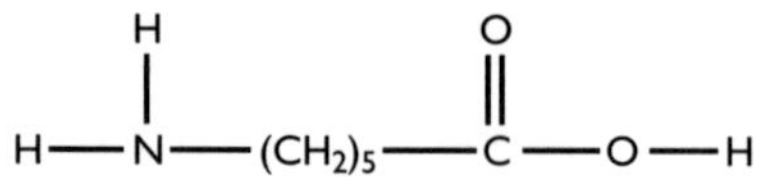

$$H-N(H)-(CH_2)_5-C(=O)-O-H$$

Hydrolysis

Hydrolysis is the reverse of condensation.

Esters

If an ester is heated under reflux with sodium hydroxide, the *sodium salt* of the *acid* and *alcohol* are formed.

If moderately concentrated HCl is used for the hydrolysis, the acid and the alcohol are formed:

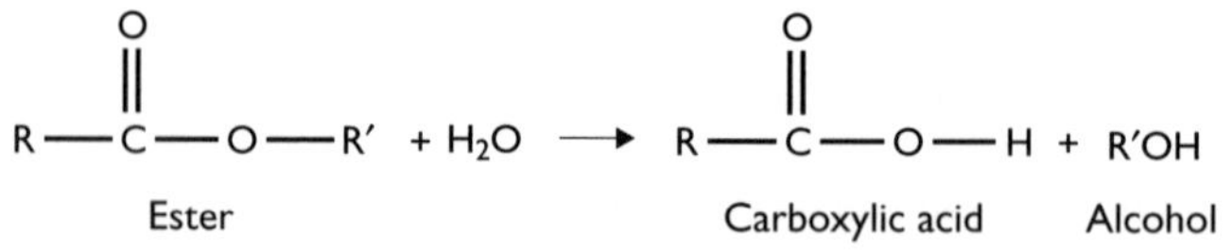

$$R-C(=O)-O-R' + H_2O \longrightarrow R-C(=O)-O-H + R'OH$$

Ester → Carboxylic acid + Alcohol

Polyesters hydrolyse to *dicarboxylic acids* and *diols*:

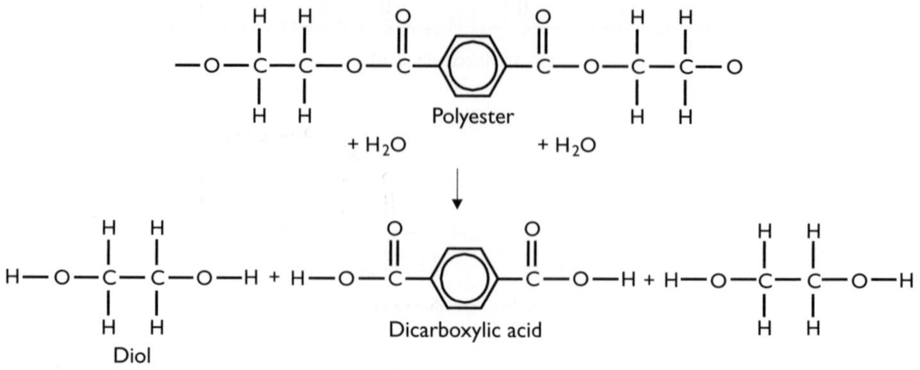

—O—CH₂—CH₂—O—C(=O)—C₆H₄—C(=O)—O—CH₂—CH₂—O—
Polyester
+ H₂O   + H₂O
↓

H—O—CH₂—CH₂—O—H + H—O—C(=O)—C₆H₄—C(=O)—O—H + H—O—CH₂—CH₂—O—H
Diol   Dicarboxylic acid

Amides

If an amide is heated under reflux with moderately concentrated acid, the *salt of the amine* and the *carboxylic acid* are formed:

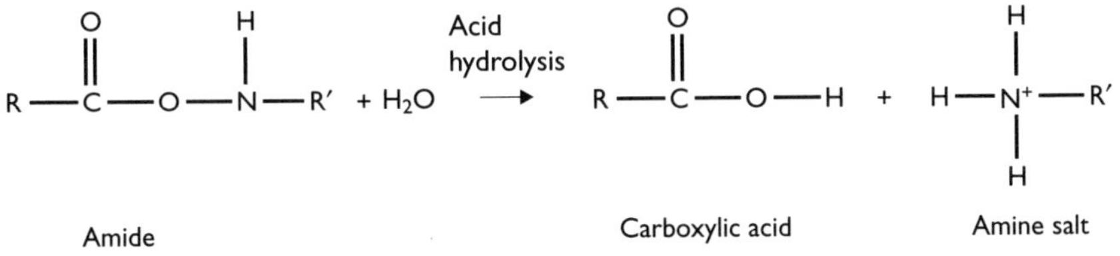

[Diagram: Amide + H₂O → Carboxylic acid + Amine salt, via Acid hydrolysis]

Heating with moderately concentrated alkali produces the *amine* and the *salt of the acid*.

So, in acid conditions, *polyamides* hydrolyse to *dicarboxylic acids* and *diamine salts*:

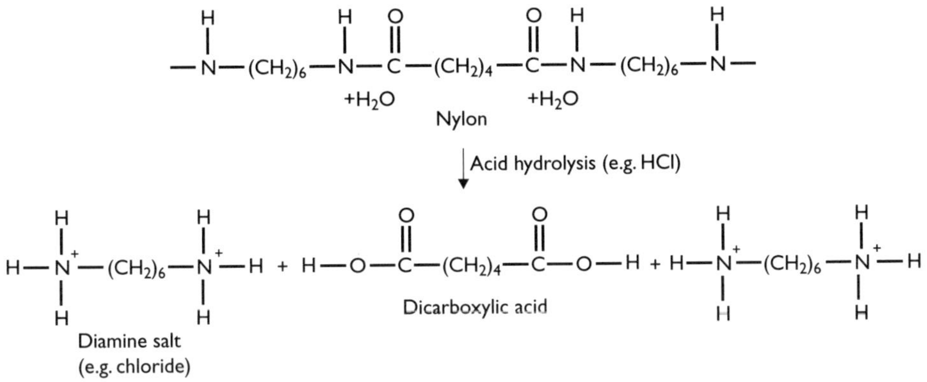

[Diagram: Nylon + H₂O undergoing Acid hydrolysis (e.g. HCl) to give Diamine salt (e.g. chloride) + Dicarboxylic acid + Diamine salt]

Properties of condensation polymers

Intermolecular forces

The three types of intermolecular force are, in decreasing order of strength, hydrogen bonds > permanent dipole–permanent dipole forces > instantaneous dipole–induced dipole forces.

- **Hydrogen bonds** occur when molecules or polymers have –OH or –NH groups, for example **nylon**.
- **Permanent dipole–permanent dipole forces** are the strongest intermolecular forces in molecules or polymers containing O or N (*without* O–H or N–H) or halogen atoms, for example **polyesters** and PVC.
- **Instantaneous dipole–induced dipole forces** are present in *all* molecules but they are usually the strongest force only when the others are absent. They are present in, for instance, poly(ethene) and poly(propene).

The strength of nylon depends partly on hydrogen bonds between adjacent chains.

The polymer *kevlar* has been designed to maximise hydrogen bonding between the chains. It is so strong that it is used for tyres and bulletproof vests. Its structure is:

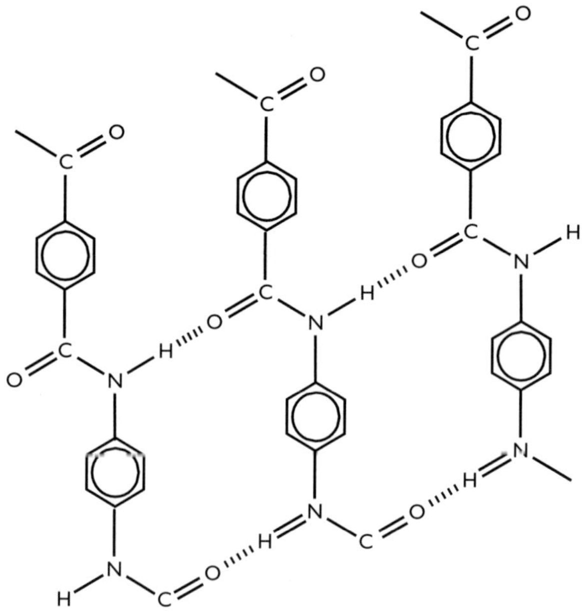

The kevlar chains are held flat by the lack of rotation of the benzene rings. The hydrogen bonds hold the flat molecules in sheets, which accounts for kevlar's strength.

The effect of heat on polymer structures

In **The polymer revolution**, you learnt about **thermoplastics** and **thermosets**. Thermosets have covalent bonds between their chains and they do not soften or melt on heating. Thermoplastics have weaker intermolecular forces between their chains and subtle changes occur when they are heated.

At low enough temperatures, all thermoplastics are **glassy**. The chains cannot move over one another and, if enough force is applied, the polymer material simply breaks.

As polymers are heated, they reach their **glass transition temperature**, T_g, above which the material becomes flexible. This temperature varies with the structure of the polymer. Eventually, on further heating, they soften and 'melt'. The temperature at which they do this is called T_m.

Polymers that have to be rigid are designed so their T_g is above room temperature, for example unplasticised PVC used for window frames. Other polymers have to be more flexible and are designed so that room temperature occurs between T_g and T_m.

The T_g is higher when:
- the *intermolecular* forces are stronger, holding the chains together
- there are *bulky side chains* which stop the chains slipping over each other

- the chains can fit together (for example, an **isotactic** structure in which all the groups are on the same side of the chain) and hence do not slide so easily because the intermolecular forces are stronger

Example: Which of two polymers is more flexible (or has lower tensile strength)?
Begin by saying polymer A is *more* flexible (has *lower* tensile strength) because its chains can move past each other more easily.

Example: Which of two polymers has a lower T_g (or T_m)?
Begin by saying polymer A has a *lower* T_g (or T_m) because its chains can move past each other more easily. Less energy is required to make the chains move.

Then explain *why* the chains move past each other more easily. Remember to compare properties each time. Three alternative approaches are given below:
- Polymer A has instantaneous dipole–induced dipole forces, whereas polymer B has stronger hydrogen bonds because...(followed by an explanation of intermolecular forces in each polymer) *or* B has more hydrogen bonds than A because...
- Polymer A has fewer/smaller side chains than polymer B, which means movement of chains is less restricted.
- Polymer A has chains that fit together poorly compared with the chains of polymer B (because...) and hence the intermolecular forces between chains are weaker.

Look for clues in the question as to which vital property to compare:
- 'In terms of intermolecular forces' means intermolecular forces should be compared.
- 'The side chains are of similar size' means side chains should *not* be compared and intermolecular forces probably *should* be compared.

Tip There are plenty of examples of these questions in past papers for you to practise!

Varying the properties

Chemists are called upon to produce polymers for different and specific functions (hence the topic title **Designer polymers**!).

First, a polymer is selected that has properties close to those required. The properties of the polymer can be changed by:
- **cold drawing**. When a polymer (above its T_g) is gently pulled, 'necking' occurs and the polymer chains line up to produce more *crystalline* regions. These regions have greater strength because of the closer packing and hence stronger intermolecular forces.

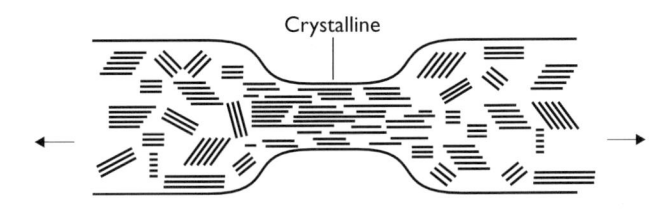

- **increasing chain length**. This increases the total number of intermolecular forces (whatever they are) and leads to stronger forces between chains, hence greater strength.
- **copolymerising**. This incorporates monomers with different functional groups into the structure, changing the polymer structure and properties. An example is the copolymerising of ethenyl ethanoate with chloroethene (the monomer of PVC).

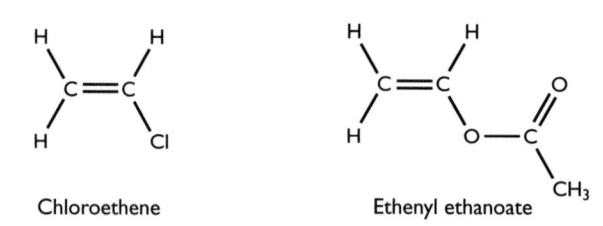

Chloroethene

Ethenyl ethanoate

Both monomers contribute permanent dipole–permanent dipole forces to the polymer, but ethenyl ethanoate has larger side groups. The occasional large side groups cause the chains to pack together less well, so the intermolecular forces are weaker and the chains can move past each other more easily. The polymer material is more flexible and has a lower T_g and T_m. The copolymer is called plasticised PVC.

It is also possible to plasticise PVC by adding a plasticiser molecule that gets between the chains and pushes them apart, to give the same effect.

Disposal of polymers

This is difficult to achieve because:
- most polymers do not degrade in the soil
- burning them wastes energy and sometimes produces toxic vapours, for example HCl from PVC
- they are hard to separate into the different types, making recycling difficult

Possible methods are:
- burning (carefully trapping toxic gases) and using the energy to generate power or as usable heat
- *cracking*, to give feedstocks for chemical processes
- *making degradable polymers*, which break down either by bacterial action or in sunlight

Proteins

This is covered in **Engineering proteins**.

Proteins are naturally occurring polymers formed by condensation polymerisation of amino acids.

Amino acids

Amino acids are the building blocks of proteins. There are 20 amino acids that make up animal proteins and they all have the same type of structure:

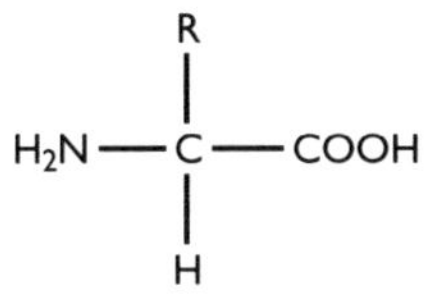

$$H_2N-\underset{\underset{H}{|}}{\overset{\overset{R}{|}}{C}}-COOH$$

In this context, the 'R-group' is *not* necessarily an alkyl group.

For example:
- if R is –H, the amino acid is called **glycine**
- if R is –CH$_2$OH, the amino acid is called **serine**

Tip You do not need to learn these names.

Properties of amino acids
Acid–base
The –NH$_2$ group is basic and the –COOH group is acidic:
 –NH$_2$ + H$^+$ ⟶ –NH$_3^+$ (this occurs when acids are added to amino acids)
 –COOH + OH$^-$ ⟶ –COO$^-$ + H$_2$O (this occurs when alkalis are added)

Both of these reactions take place *within* an amino acid molecule, forming a **zwitterion**:

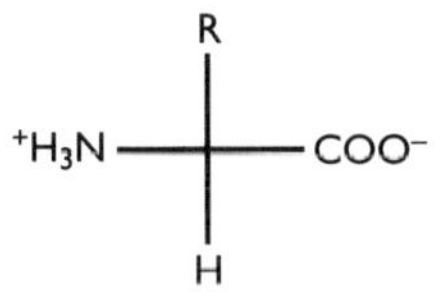

$$^+H_3N-\underset{\underset{H}{|}}{\overset{\overset{R}{|}}{|}}-COO^-$$

This explains why solid amino acids have high melting points and why they are very soluble in water. The solution is nearly neutral unless there are extra –COOH or –NH$_2$ groups.

Optical isomerism
All the amino acids (except glycine) have *four different groups* around the central carbon and thus show *optical isomerism* (see page 18).

Protein structure

Primary structure
This consists of amino acids joined together by secondary amide links (see page 15). In the context of proteins, these links are called *peptide links*.

The diagram below shows glycine and alanine (R group, CH$_3$) joining together to form part of a protein. This is a *condensation reaction* — water is eliminated.

A2 Chemistry

Part of the primary structure of a protein

Two amino acids combined together are called a **dipeptide** (even though there is only *one* peptide link!).

The sequence of amino acids in a protein structure is called its **primary structure**. The primary structure is characteristic of the particular protein. It determines the way the protein folds, for example whether it is designed to be a **fibrous structural** protein (like those in hair or fingernails) or a **globular** protein such as an **enzyme**.

The amino acids present in a protein can be identified as follows:
- Heat a sample of the protein under reflux with moderately concentrated hydrochloric acid. This *hydrolyses* it into its individual amino acids.
- Spot the resulting mixture onto chromatography paper.
- Run the chromatogram using a suitable solvent.
- Use a **locating agent** (ninhydrin), followed by warming in an oven, to make the spots visible.

The amino acids can be identified either by running known amino acids alongside and comparing which move to the same height, or by measuring R_f values:

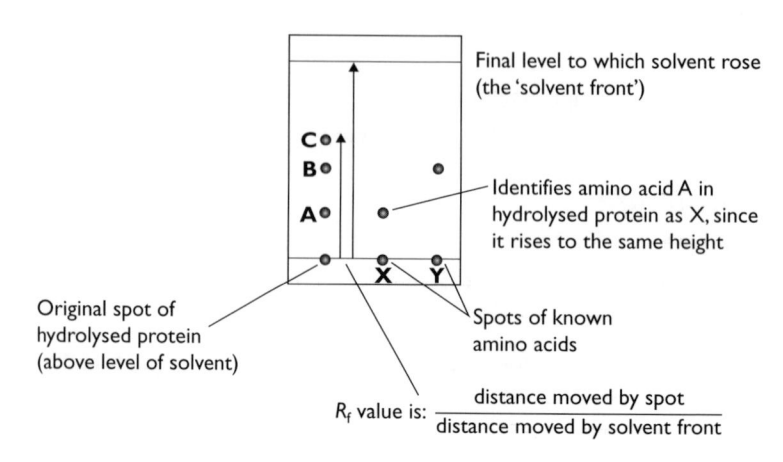

R_f value is: $\dfrac{\text{distance moved by spot}}{\text{distance moved by solvent front}}$

Secondary structure

This describes how the amino acid chain folds. There are two possible folding patterns, the **helix** and the **sheet**. Secondary structures are held together by **hydrogen bonds** between the C=O groups and N–H groups, as shown in the diagrams below.

Helix

Sheet

Tertiary structure

This is how portions of helices and/or sheets fold up further to give the overall shape of the protein. Fibrous proteins, such as the hair protein keratin, have a tertiary structure consisting of many helices wound together, in a similar way to pieces of thread being wound together to make string. Globular proteins, such as enzymes, have a mixture of helices and sheets in their structure:

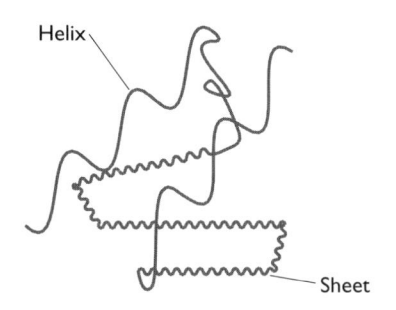

Helix

Sheet

The tertiary structure is held together by various types of interaction, which are shown in the diagram below. However, this is schematic — you would not expect to find so many different forces so close together!

| Covalent bonds 'disulphide bridges' | Ionic interactions | Hydrogen bonds | Instantaneous dipole–induced dipole forces |

Quaternary structure

Some proteins have several distinct tertiary units connected together, often as ligands (see page 41) to a metal ion. For example, the protein insulin is a **hexamer**. This is known as the quaternary structure.

Enzymes

Enzymes are **biological catalysts** present in all living systems. They are used industrially in a variety of important processes, for example brewing, wine making and cheese making. They are also used in washing powders.

The tertiary structure of an enzyme is folded to form a cleft in the molecule with a specific shape into which the **substrate** molecule fits. (The substrate is the molecule whose reactions are being catalysed.) This cleft is called the **active site**. Within the active site, important R-groups on the protein chain are held in position by the tertiary structure and bind the substrate to the enzyme.

The substrate binds by weak intermolecular forces to the active site, forming an **enzyme–substrate complex**. Here, bond enthalpies are changed and reactions occur which normally require much greater activation enthalpies.

The products do not fit the active site and bind less well, so they leave. The enzyme is now able to catalyse the reaction of a further substrate molecule.

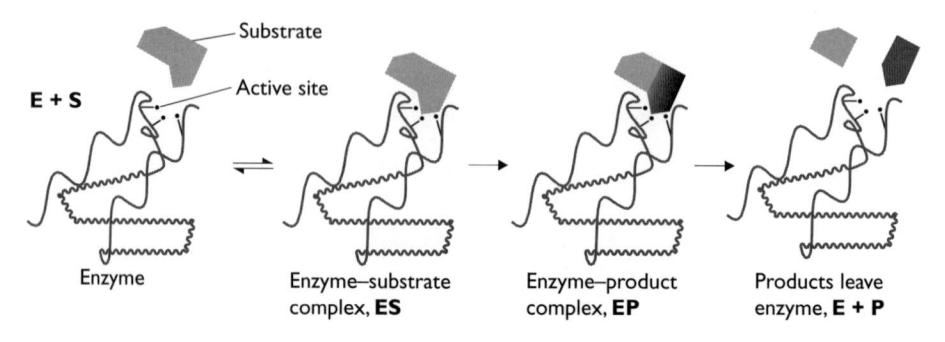

E + S (Enzyme) ⇌ Enzyme–substrate complex, **ES** → Enzyme–product complex, **EP** → Products leave enzyme, **E + P**

OCR *(Salters)* Unit 2849

Characteristics of enzyme reactions
Enzymes are:
- *specific*. In order to fit and bind onto the active site, the substrate molecule must be exactly the right shape. When the substrate is a chiral molecule, often only the reaction of *one* enantiomer is catalysed.
- *sensitive to pH*. pH affects the ratio of COO^- to NH^+ present in R-groups. Small changes in pH can affect the charges on the R-groups present in the active site, resulting in a decrease in activity. A change in pH of more than two units causes the tertiary structure of an enzyme to break down, with the loss of the active site. This is called **denaturation**.
- *sensitive to temperature*. As the temperature of an enzyme-catalysed reaction is raised, the reaction gets faster, as with all other reactions. However, above a certain temperature, the activity falls rapidly to zero as the enzyme becomes denatured. In this case, the molecular agitation caused by the increasing temperature breaks the hydrogen bonds holding together the secondary and tertiary structures.
- *inhibited* by substances that bind irreversibly to the active site, such as heavy metal ions. Substances that resemble substrate molecules also inhibit enzymes. Substrate and inhibitor compete for occupancy of the active site. However, once in the active site, inhibitors do not react. Substrate molecules cannot enter, so the reaction rate slows down. For example, the enzyme succinate dehydrogenase catalyses the oxidation of butanedioic (succinic) acid by removing hydrogen:

$$HOOC-CH_2-CH_2-COOH \longrightarrow HOOC-CH=CH-COOH + H_2$$

The enzyme is inhibited by propanedioic acid, $HOOC-CH_2-COOH$ which can bind to the active site but has no CH_2-CH_2 link from which hydrogen can be removed.

At high substrate concentrations, enzyme-catalysed reactions are **zero-order** with respect to substrate concentration (see pages 36–37).

Genes and protein synthesis

You meet this topic in **Engineering proteins**.

DNA

DNA, which stands for deoxyribonucleic acid, carries the code to make proteins. Since enzymes are proteins, this means DNA controls all our bodily functions. A segment of DNA responsible for the production of a protein is called a **gene**.

DNA has a **double helix** structure. (Note that it is *not* a protein!) Each strand has a 'sugar–phosphate' backbone. The sugar is deoxyribose. Attached to each sugar is a 'base', denoted by the letters T, A, G and C (thymine, adenine, guanine and cytosine). These hydrogen-bond in pairs — T with A and C with G — which is how the two strands of the helix are held together.

A2 Chemistry

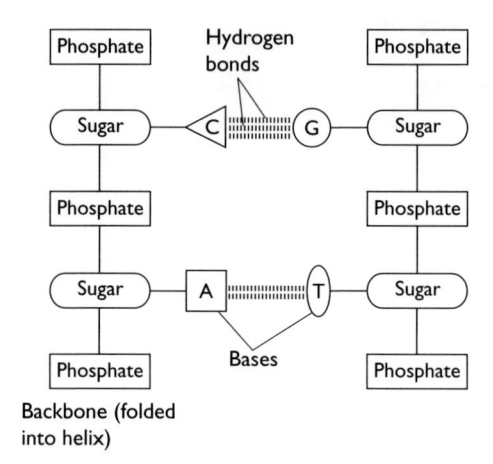

[Diagram: DNA backbone structure showing Phosphate–Sugar–Phosphate–Sugar–Phosphate on each side, with bases C–G and A–T paired in the middle via hydrogen bonds. Labelled: Backbone (folded into helix), Bases, Hydrogen bonds.]

Tip This is all the detail you need to learn. You do not need to learn the names of the bases.

The fact that the bases pair up is important in that during cell division, each DNA molecule **replicates**. Hydrogen bonds between the strands break and each strand acts as a template for the synthesis of a new strand. In this way, the genetic code is passed on as cells divide.

Protein synthesis

RNA stands for **ribonucleic acid**. RNA has the base U (uracil) instead of T; U pairs with A. It also has ribose as the sugar instead of deoxyribose. During protein synthesis, **messenger RNA** is produced by the genes in a similar way to that in which DNA replicates itself. The messenger RNA carries the code from the DNA in the nucleus to the **ribosomes**, which are in the cytoplasm outside the nucleus. Protein synthesis occurs in the ribosomes.

Messenger RNA is a single-stranded molecule. Each group of *three bases* is called a **codon** because it codes for an amino acid. In the cytoplasm of the cell, each amino acid has its own **transfer RNA** molecule with an **anticodon**, which has bases complementary to those of a particular codon. The transfer RNA molecules bring the amino acids to the ribosomes. As the ribosome moves along the messenger RNA, each anticodon forms hydrogen bonds with the corresponding codon. In this way, the primary structure of the protein is assembled in the right order, so that the protein can fold into its correct shape.

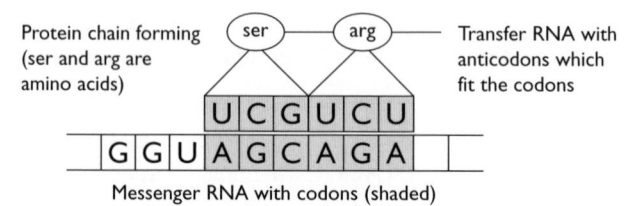

[Diagram: Protein chain forming (ser and arg are amino acids) — ser and arg connected to anticodons UCG and UCU, which pair with messenger RNA codons GGU AGC AGA. Transfer RNA with anticodons which fit the codons. Messenger RNA with codons (shaded).]

Tip You only need to know the ideas here, not the detail.

OCR *(Salters)* Unit 2849

Genetic engineering

We now know the base sequence of many genes and therefore the amino acid sequences of the proteins they code for. We can extract genes from some organisms. Moving a gene from one organism into another is called **genetic engineering**.

Bacteria are often used to make proteins using the following method:
- The required gene is cut from the organism's DNA, using **restriction enzymes**.
- Rings of DNA called **plasmids** are extracted from the bacterial cells.
- The plasmids are cut, using restriction enzymes, and the new gene is **spliced** in, using other enzymes.
- The modified plasmids are replaced in the bacterial cells.
- When the bacterial cells multiply in a fermenter, they pass on the new gene.
- The gene causes synthesis of the required protein, which is then extracted from the contents of the fermenter.

Uses of genetic engineering
These include:
- making proteins, such as human insulin, using the method described above
- modifying the structure of a protein, for example by changing a single amino acid to stop insulin molecules grouping together
- modifying human and animal genes using gene therapy, for example as a possible cure for cystic fibrosis
- modifying plants by changing their properties, for instance improving taste, yield, and resistance to spoilage
- producing plants that synthesise insecticides

Arguments against genetic engineering
Some people oppose the technique because, for example:
- it might produce 'superbugs' with resistance to all known antibiotics
- the plant genes might transfer to other species, for example weeds, which would then have resistance to insects

Making medicines

From the identification of a possible new medicine to its final launch takes about 14 years and costs up to £100 million pounds. The process involves:
- determining molecular structures
- modifying molecular structures to give:
  - greater effectiveness
  - effectiveness over longer periods
  - fewer side effects
  - lower toxicity in an overdose
  - fewer groups who may be allergic to it
  - fewer addictive effects
  - the most suitable form for administration to the patient (e.g. pills)
  - fewer reactions with other medicines

- trials, culminating in human tests to determine the above and also on 'at risk' groups such as:
  - children
  - old people
  - pregnant women
  - those with allergies

Equilibrium

Revision

This summarises what you have learnt about equilibrium in **The atmosphere**. You are expected to use that information in this unit.

A chemical equilibrium is represented as shown below:

$$I_2(aq) + 2OH^-(aq) \rightleftharpoons I^-(aq) + IO^-(aq) + H_2O(l)$$

This means that, once an **equilibrium position** has been reached:
- the *concentrations* of all reactants and products are *constant* (*rarely equal* and *never zero*!)
- the equilibrium is *dynamic*, that is, the forward and back reactions both proceed but at equal rates, resulting in no apparent change. The *forward* reaction goes left to right and the *back* reaction right to left.

It is possible to change the position of equilibrium by changing the concentrations of reagents or products, the temperature or, in the case of a gas reaction, the pressure.

A rule that can be used to predict what happens when the conditions are changed (but not to *explain* it) is **Le Chatelier's principle**. This states that *if a change is applied to a system at equilibrium, the system will adjust to oppose that change*.

If the *concentration* of a substance on the left is increased, the equilibrium position will move 'to the right', i.e. more products will be formed and the concentrations of the reactants will fall.

The equilibrium constant, K_c

You meet this in **Engineering proteins**.

For the reaction $N_2(g) + 3H_2(g) \rightleftharpoons 2NH_3(g)$:

$$K_c = \frac{[NH_3]^2}{[N_2][H_2]^3}$$

- Square brackets represent concentrations in $mol\,dm^{-3}$.
- The equilibrium constant has *product(s) over reactants*.

- Concentrations are raised to the powers of the number of molecules in the equation.
- The terms are multiplied, *never* added!

Units of K_c

These depend on the particular reaction. The best way to work out the units is to substitute M for $mol\,dm^{-3}$. Then the Ms can be cancelled and what remains translated back to powers of $mol\,dm^{-3}$. Thus, for the ammonia reaction, the units are:

$$\frac{M^2}{M \times M^3} = M^{-2}$$

M^{-2} can be written as $(mol\,dm^{-3})^{-2}$ but it is expanded to $mol^{-2}\,dm^6$.

Example

In an equilibrium mixture of nitrogen, hydrogen and ammonia, the concentrations of hydrogen and ammonia are $0.40\,mol\,dm^{-3}$ and $0.0080\,mol\,dm^{-3}$ respectively. K_c at the temperature of the mixture is $4.0 \times 10^{-2}\,mol^{-2}\,dm^6$. Calculate the concentration of nitrogen.

From the equation above:

$$[N_2] = \frac{[NH_3]^2}{K_c \times [H_2]^3} = \frac{0.0080^2}{4.0 \times 10^{-2} \times 0.40^3} = 2.5 \times 10^{-2}\,mol\,dm^{-3}$$

Tip Try this yourself, to make sure that you know which buttons to press on your calculator!

The effect of temperature and pressure

Le Chatelier's principle can be applied to changes of temperature and pressure.

- If the *temperature* is increased, the equilibrium will move in the *endothermic* direction (opposing the increased temperature by cooling the surroundings). For example:

    $N_2(g) + 3H_2(g) \rightleftharpoons 2NH_3(g)$ $\Delta H = -92\,kJ\,mol^{-1}$

    Increasing the temperature will shift the equilibrium position in the *endothermic* direction, that is, lowering the amount of ammonia.

- If the *pressure* is increased on an equilibrium involving gases, the equilibrium will move in the direction of *fewer gas molecules* (opposing the increased pressure by lowering the pressure). For example:

    $N_2(g) + 3H_2(g) \rightleftharpoons 2NH_3(g)$

    Increasing the pressure will shift the equilibrium position in the direction of *fewer molecules,* that is, to produce *more* ammonia.

Note that if there are equal numbers of moles on each side of the equation, changing the pressure will have no effect on the equilibrium position, for example:

$H_2 + I_2 \rightleftharpoons 2HI$

Note that *temperature* changes achieve their effect by changing the **equilibrium constant**. However, *pressure* changes do not change the equilibrium constant, nor do changes in concentration.

A2 Chemistry

Condition	Effect on equilibrium position	Effect on equilibrium constant
Increasing temperature	Moves in endothermic direction	Changes to allow change of equilibrium position
Increasing pressure	Move in direction of fewer gas molecules	No change
Adding a catalyst	None (catalyses the forward and the back reactions equally)	No change

Reaction rates

Rate of reaction at a given moment is defined as the change in concentration divided by the time taken for the change.

Effect of concentration

Rate equation and rate constant
The rate equation for a reaction A + B ⟶ products is:
$$\text{rate} = k[A]^a[B]^b$$
where k is the **rate constant**, square brackets represent concentrations in mol dm^{-3} and a and b are the **orders of reaction** with respect to A and B respectively. (The overall order of reaction is $a + b$.)

Units of the rate constant
The units of rate are $\text{mol dm}^{-3}\,\text{s}^{-1}$. Thus, for an overall first-order reaction:
$$k = \frac{\text{rate}}{[\text{reagent}]} \quad \left(\text{units} = \frac{\text{mol dm}^{-3}\,\text{s}^{-1}}{\text{mol dm}^{-3}} = \mathbf{s^{-1}}\right)$$

For a second-order reaction:
$$k = \frac{\text{rate}}{[\text{reagent}]^2} \quad \left(\text{units} = \frac{\text{mol dm}^{-3}\,\text{s}^{-1}}{\text{mol}^2\,\text{dm}^{-6}} = \mathbf{mol^{-1}\,dm^3\,s^{-1}}\right)$$

Measuring orders of reaction
Orders of reaction have nothing to do with the overall balanced chemical equation for the reaction because this usually represents a series of steps. Orders must be measured by experiment.

Method 1
This method involves measuring the time for the initial part of the reaction to occur. This may involve measuring a colour change. The reciprocal of the time taken (1/time) is proportional to the *initial* rate, which applies when the reactants' concentrations have their starting values. For example, if three reagents, A, B and C, react, the initial rates are measured at different starting concentrations:

OCR (Salters) Unit 2849

Tube	[A]	[B]	[C]	Relative rate
1	1	1	1	1
2	2	1	1	1
3	1	2	1	2
4	1	1	2	4

- Comparing tube 2 with tube 1 — the concentration of A has doubled and the rate has remained the same. This means that the order of reaction is **zero** with respect to A.
- Tubes 1 and 3 show that the rate doubles when the concentration of B doubles, so the reaction is **first** order with respect to B.
- Tubes 1 and 4 show that the reaction is **second** order with respect to C, since the rate goes up by four when the concentration of C doubles.

Method 2

This involves following the reaction to completion. The reaction is followed by either:
- measuring the concentration of a reactant or product against time, or
- measuring a property that is proportional to the concentration, such as colour intensity, pH or volume of gas evolved

One reagent is **limiting** (at a smaller concentration than the others) and a graph is plotted of this reactant's concentration against time. If the **half-life** (see below) is constant, the reaction is first-order with respect to the limiting reagent. If the graph is a straight line, the reaction is zero-order. If successive half-lives increase, it is second-order. For example, the graph below shows the variation in the concentration of X with time:

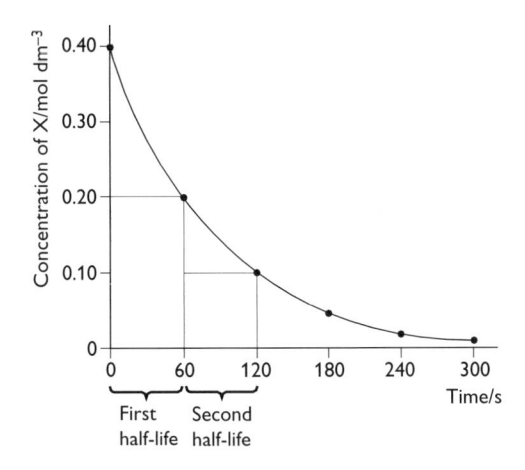

The first half-life is the time taken for the concentration to fall to half its initial value, that is, from 0.4 to 0.2. The second half-life is the time taken to fall from 0.2 to 0.1. They are both 60 seconds, so the reaction is first-order with respect to X.

When plotting graphs and working out half-lives:
- choose scales carefully, to make plotting easy
- label axes fully (don't forget powers of ten and units)
- plot points carefully and accurately, in pencil
- carefully draw the best smooth curve through the points in pencil (*practise this!*)
- show half-life working on the graph, as above

Reaction mechanisms

Many reactions occur in several steps. The slowest step (like a 'bottleneck') is called the **rate-determining step**. If a reactant is used in a fast step *after* the rate-determining step, then its concentration will not affect the overall rate of the reaction — the overall reaction will be *zero-order* with respect to that reactant.

Enzyme kinetics

Enzyme reactions occur as follows:
  Step 1: $E + S \rightleftharpoons ES$
  Step 2: $ES \longrightarrow E + P$
(See page 30.)

At *low substrate concentrations*, step 1 is rate-determining. Thus, the reaction is *first-order* with respect to both enzyme and substrate.

However, enzymes are molecules with large M_r values, so their molar concentrations can be very small. As the substrate concentration rises, it becomes very much greater than the enzyme concentration. The enzyme is then said to be **saturated**, with all active sites occupied. Therefore, under these conditions, the enzyme is almost always in an enzyme–substrate complex. This results in **step 2** becoming rate-determining. The reaction is *zero-order* with respect to the substrate concentration, though still first-order with respect to enzyme concentration.

Effect of pressure, surface area, temperature and catalysts

This is revision of work done in **The atmosphere**. You are expected to use the information in this unit.
- Rates of reaction are affected by **pressure** (for a gas reaction) and **surface area** (for a reaction involving a solid). The rate increases as the pressure rises or surface area increases, since the *number of collisions per second* goes up.
- Rates of reaction are affected by **temperature** in a rather more complicated way. Although increasing the temperature affects the number of collisions per second, of far more importance is its effect on the *number of molecules colliding with energy greater than the activation enthalpy*. The **activation enthalpy** is the minimum energy that two molecules need in order to react when they collide.
- Rates of reaction are affected by the presence of **catalysts**. A catalyst speeds up a chemical reaction but is unchanged chemically at the end. It takes part in the reaction sequence but is regenerated. Catalysts work by *lowering the activation enthalpy* of a reaction and so they also increase the value of the rate constant, k. They do this by providing an *alternative route* for the reaction.

OCR(Salters) Unit 2849

In your course so far, you will have come across two kinds of catalyst:
- **Homogeneous** catalysts. These are in the same physical state as the reactants, for example chlorine atoms catalysing the breakdown of ozone in the stratosphere.
- **Heterogeneous** catalysts. These are in a different physical state from the reactants, for example solid catalysts used in a catalytic converter to speed up gas reactions. The reactants are **adsorbed** (chemically bound) onto the catalyst surface where bond breaking and making occurs and the products diffuse away from the surface.

Catalyst poisons are adsorbed on to the surface of such catalysts, stopping the catalyst working.

Transition metals

Electronic structure

Transition elements lie in the d-block of the periodic table where the **d sub-shell** is the one being filled. Given the atomic number, you are only expected to be able to work out from the atomic number the electronic structures of the *first row* of d-block elements, from scandium to zinc.

After argon ($1s^22s^22p^63s^23p^6$), the next element (potassium) starts to fill the $4s$ sub-shell, since the $3d$ sub-shell is slightly above it in terms of energy. However, after calcium ($1s^22s^22p^63s^23p^64s^2$), the $3d$ sub-shell starts to fill. Thus, the electronic structure of scandium can be written either as $1s^22s^22p^63s^23p^63d^14s^2$ or as $[Ar]3d^14s^2$, where [Ar] represents the electronic structure of argon. Alternatively, the 'electron box' representation can be used. Each box represents an **orbital** (named from the time when people thought that electrons orbited round the nucleus).

Element	Atomic number	spdf description	Electron box description 3d orbitals 4s orbital	Notes
Sc	21	$[Ar]3d^14s^2$	↑ ☐ ☐ ☐ ☐ ↑↓	Sc^{3+} is the only ion with [Ar] structure*
Ti	22	$[Ar]3d^24s^2$	↑ ↑ ☐ ☐ ☐ ↑↓	
V	23	$[Ar]3d^34s^2$	↑ ↑ ↑ ☐ ☐ ↑↓	
Cr	24	$[Ar]3d^54s^1$	↑ ↑ ↑ ↑ ↑ ↑	Does not follow pattern**
Mn	25	$[Ar]3d^54s^2$	↑ ↑ ↑ ↑ ↑ ↑↓	
Fe	26	$[Ar]3d^64s^2$	↑↓ ↑ ↑ ↑ ↑ ↑↓	

39

Element	Atomic number	spdf description	Electron box description (3d orbitals, 4s orbital)	Notes
Co	27	[Ar]3d⁷4s²		
Ni	28	[Ar]3d⁸4s²		
Cu	29	[Ar]3d¹⁰4s¹		Does not follow pattern**
Zn	30	[Ar]3d¹⁰4s²		Zn²⁺ is the only ion with [Ar]3d¹⁰ structure*

* The definition of a **transition metal** is an element that forms at least one ion with a partially filled d sub-shell of electrons. Scandium and zinc do not meet this definition. Therefore, they are d-block elements but *not* transition metals.

** d^5 and d^{10} are particularly stable electron arrangements. Therefore, chromium and copper have the electron arrangements shown above, with $4s^1$; not $4s^2$.

Ions are formed by losing the $4s$ electrons first, then the d electrons. For example, Fe^{2+} is $[Ar]3d^6$ and Fe^{3+} is $[Ar]3d^5$. Cu^{2+} is $[Ar]3d^9$.

Typical properties

Variable oxidation state

The only ion formed by magnesium is Mg^{2+}, because the most stable electron arrangement is [Ne]. However, within the $3d$ and $4s$ sub-shells, there are usually several stable electron arrangements, resulting in several oxidation states. The only oxidation states you need to *learn* are those given in the table and notes above.

Formation of complexes

A **complex** is a metal atom or ion surrounded by **ligands**. Ligands are negative ions or neutral molecules with a lone pair of electrons, which they can donate to metal ions to form complexes.

Ligand	Example of complex	Charge on metal ion/atom	Charge on complex
H_2O	$[Fe(H_2O)_6]^{3+}$	+3	+3; ligand is neutral
NH_3	$[Ni(NH_3)_6]^{2+}$	+2	+2; ligand is neutral
CN^-	$[Fe(CN)_6]^{3-}$	+3	−3; ligand has charge of −1
Cl^-	$[CuCl_4]^{2-}$	+2	−2; ligand has charge of −1
CO	$Ni(CO)_4$	0	0; this is a complex but not a complex ion — you will seldom meet these!

Tip You need to know that these are ligands and how the charges balance.

OCR (Salters) Unit 2849

Note the use of square brackets to surround a complex ion.

Bonding in complexes is a mixture of **dative covalent** bonding and **ionic attraction**. The dative covalent bonding is explained by the ligands having lone pairs of electrons and the transition metals having empty *d* orbitals into which electrons can be donated.

Polydentate ligands

Polydentate means 'lots of teeth' and applies to ligands that can attach to the central metal ion from more than one part of the ligand. The example you need to know about is **edta^{4-}**. The letters 'edta' represent the old name for the ion.

Its structure is:

There are *six* positions within this flexible ligand that can attach to a central metal ion, using the lone pairs on the two N atoms and on the four O$^-$ ions.

Shapes of complexes

The shape is determined by the **coordination number** of the central atom or ion, that is, the *number of ligands that surround it*. The coordination numbers you need to know about are 4 and 6.

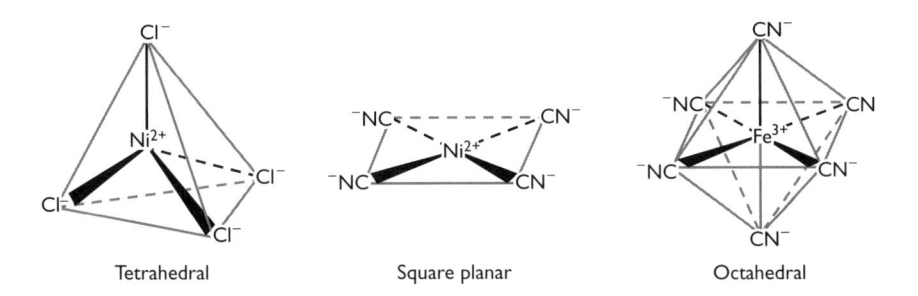

Tetrahedral   Square planar   Octahedral

Ligand exchange

This occurs when a transition metal ion swaps one ligand or set of ligands for another, for example:

$[Ni(H_2O)_6]^{2+} + 6NH_3 \rightleftharpoons [Ni(NH_3)_6]^{2+} + 6H_2O$

Here the Ni^{2+} ion has exchanged six water molecules for six ammonia molecules.

The **stability constant** for $[Ni(NH_3)_6]^{2+}$ is:

$$K_{stab} = \frac{[[Ni(NH_3)_6]^{2+}]}{[[Ni(H_2O)_6]^{2+}] \times [NH_3]^6}$$

Note that this is the same as the **equilibrium constant** for this reaction (see page 34), except that the concentration of water, which will be large and virtually constant, has been included in K_{stab}. Note also that square brackets are used here to show concentrations and also to show the complex ions. Try not to be confused by this.

Stability constants measure how stable a complex ion is compared with the complex having the same central ion and water as the ligand. Because the numbers are often large, the log of K_{stab} is usually given. (You will learn more about logs when you study pH in **The oceans**.) For the above reaction, the numerical value of K_{stab} is 1×10^8, so $\log K_{stab} = 8$.

For the nickel–edta complex, $[Ni(edta)]^{2-}$, $\log K_{stab} = 19$. This means that edta will replace ammonia ligands. However, ammonia ligands will not replace edta ligands because $[Ni(edta)]^{2-}$ is so much more stable, as shown by the values of K_{stab}.

Formation of coloured ions in solution

The presence of ligands around the central ion affects the electrons in the d sub-shell. The five d orbitals are split into two groups at different energy levels. The energy difference between the split energy levels often corresponds to a frequency of visible light ($\Delta E = h\nu$).

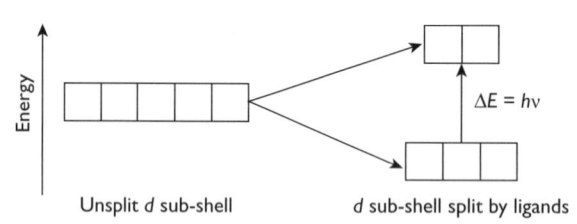

When electrons are excited from a lower energy level to a higher one, visible light of a particular frequency band is absorbed. The frequencies *not* absorbed are transmitted and the compound is seen as the complementary colour. For example, a compound that absorbs red and yellow light looks blue. An **absorption spectrum** shows the colours absorbed.

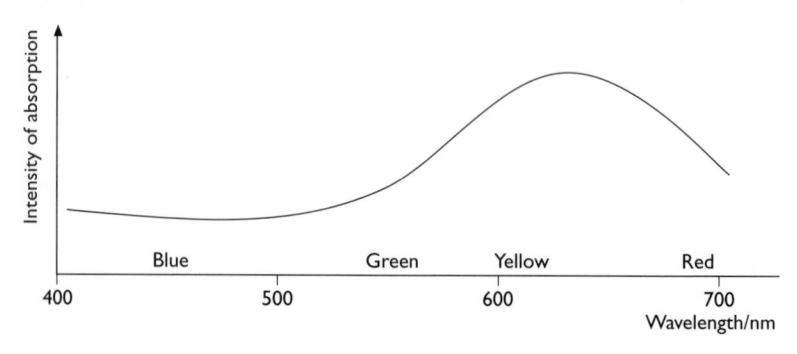

OCR*(Salters)* Unit 2849

Some reactions with a colour change are given in the table below.

Ion	Reaction with NaOH(aq) and small amounts of NH$_3$(aq)	Observation	Reaction with excess NH$_3$(aq)
Cu^{2+}	Cu^{2+}(aq) + 2OH$^-$(aq) ⟶ Cu(OH)$_2$(s)	Light blue precipitate	Precipitate dissolves to give a dark blue solution of [Cu(NH$_3$)$_4$]$^{2+}$(aq)
Fe^{2+}	Fe^{2+}(aq) + 2OH$^-$(aq) ⟶ Fe(OH)$_2$(s)	Dark green precipitate	No change
Fe^{3+}	Fe^{3+}(aq) + 3OH$^-$(aq) ⟶ Fe(OH)$_3$(s)	Rust-coloured precipitate	No change

The reactions are initially the same with both aqueous sodium hydroxide and aqueous ammonia, as the latter contains OH$^-$ ions. Excess ammonia forms a complex with copper ions but not with iron(II) or iron(III) ions.

Tip You need to learn all the reactions in the above table.

Catalytic behaviour
(See page 38 for more on catalysts.)

Many catalysts are either transition metals or their compounds. They work as catalysts because:
- they have unfilled *d* sub-shells. Thus, their surfaces can easily **adsorb** (form bonds with) gas molecules in **heterogeneous catalysis**. Examples are the use of iron in the Haber process and the use of platinum in the hydrogenation of alkenes.
- they have variable oxidation states. This enables them to work as both **homogeneous** and **heterogeneous catalysts**. For example, in the reaction A + B ⟶ C + D, a faster route might be:
  A + reduced X ⟶ C + oxidised X
  B + oxidised X ⟶ D + reduced X

Either reduced X or oxidised X will act as a catalyst.

Steel

Types of steel
Steel is iron containing small amounts of carbon and other elements. Addition of:
- 1% carbon leads to a steel of high tensile strength (e.g. for drill bits)
- 0.1% carbon leads to steel that is much more **ductile** ('bendy' — e.g. for paper clips)
- chromium and nickel make **stainless steel** which is much less prone to rusting
- aluminium makes steel harder, though it can still be shaped

Tip Learn these (or other) examples.

Making steel

Here are the essential steps in the **BOS (basic oxygen steelmaking) process** for making steel from molten iron, usually from a mixture of scrap steel and blast furnace iron.

- Sulphur is removed by adding magnesium to the molten iron, producing magnesium sulphide which is raked off the surface.

    $Mg + S \longrightarrow MgS$

- Blowing oxygen through the molten iron oxidises the elements present, including Fe (but only a small proportion as there is so much of it!). Oxidation of carbon is vital because it lowers the carbon content.

    $2C + O_2 \longrightarrow 2CO$

    The toxic CO is collected and used as a fuel. The other elements present are mostly non-metals and are oxidised to *acidic* oxides, for example:

    $4P + 5O_2 \longrightarrow P_4O_{10}$
    $Si + O_2 \longrightarrow SiO_2$

- A mixture of the *bases* CaO and MgO is added, to react with the acidic oxides.

    $SiO_2 + CaO \longrightarrow CaSiO_3$

    $CaSiO_3$ is the main ingredient of **slag**.

- Elements are added back to make steel of the required specification.

Recycling steel

- Steel can be easily separated from other metals because most types of steel are magnetic.
- Scrap steel can be melted as part of the raw material for the BOS process.
- A problem sometimes arises through unwanted elements present in the scrap.
- Tin-plated cans are treated with hot sodium hydroxide solution to remove the tin.

Redox

Revision

The chemical ideas here are from **Minerals to elements**.

Definitions

- Oxidation is *loss* of electrons.
- Reduction is *gain* of electrons.

Remember either *OIL RIG* (**o**xidation **is** **l**oss, **r**eduction **is** **g**ain) or *LEO the lion goes GER* (**l**oss of **e**lectrons is **o**xidation, **g**ain of **e**lectrons is **r**eduction).

Oxidation states

- The oxidation states of the atoms in a *molecule* (of neutral charge) add to zero. This means that the oxidation state of an atom in an *element* is always *zero*.
- The oxidation states of the atoms in an *ion* add to the charge on the ion.

There are certain fixed oxidation states for atoms in compounds:

Element	Oxidation state	Comments
H	+1	Except in H$^-$
O	−2	Except in peroxides (−1) and fluorine compounds
F	−1	
Cl	−1	Except in compounds with O or F
Group 1	+1	
Group 2	+2	

Example

Species	Positive oxidation states	Negative oxidation states	Sum of oxidation states
SO_3	S; +6	O; 3 × −2	0
PCl_5	P; +5	Cl; 5 × −1	0
SO_4^{2-}	S; +6	O; 4 × −2	−2
NH_4^+	H; 4 × +1	N; −3	+1
N_2	N; 0		0

Tip Don't forget the sign (even when positive), followed by the number.

- When the oxidation state of an atom *increases*, it has been *oxidised*.
- When the oxidation state of an atom *decreases*, it has been *reduced*.

Half-equations

These show the electrons being transferred. For example, the reaction between copper metal and silver ions involves the loss of two electrons from each copper atom and the gain of one electron each by the silver ions:

$Cu(s) + 2Ag^+(aq) \longrightarrow Cu^{2+}(aq) + 2Ag(s)$

The half-equations are:

$Cu(s) \longrightarrow Cu^{2+}(aq) + 2e^-$ (loss of electrons is *oxidation*)

$Ag^+(aq) + e^- \longrightarrow Ag(s)$ (gain of electrons is *reduction*)

Other examples of half-equations are:

$2Cl^-(aq) \longrightarrow Cl_2(aq) + 2e^-$ (*oxidation* of chloride to chlorine)

$MnO_4^-(aq) + 8H^+(aq) + 5e^- \longrightarrow Mn^{2+}(aq) + 4H_2O(l)$
   (*reduction* of manganate(VII) to manganese(II))

Note that the number of electrons transferred is equal to the oxidation state change each time.

(Half-equations can be added together to make full equations — see page 49.)

Cells and electrode potentials

A piece of zinc is placed in some zinc(II) solution.

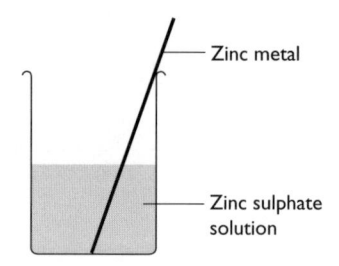

Zinc metal

Zinc sulphate solution

There is an exchange of electrons, represented by the half-equation:

$$Zn(s) \rightleftharpoons Zn^{2+}(aq) + 2e^-$$

This equilibrium is set up after a short while — the electrons going into the metal rod.

Another beaker contains a piece of copper in contact with copper(II) ions. An equilibrium is again set up:

$$Cu(s) \rightleftharpoons Cu^{2+}(aq) + 2e^-$$

Our knowledge of chemistry leads us to expect that the zinc equilibrium will lie further to the right than that for copper, since zinc is the more reactive metal. We can test this by putting the two **half-cells** together to make a cell:

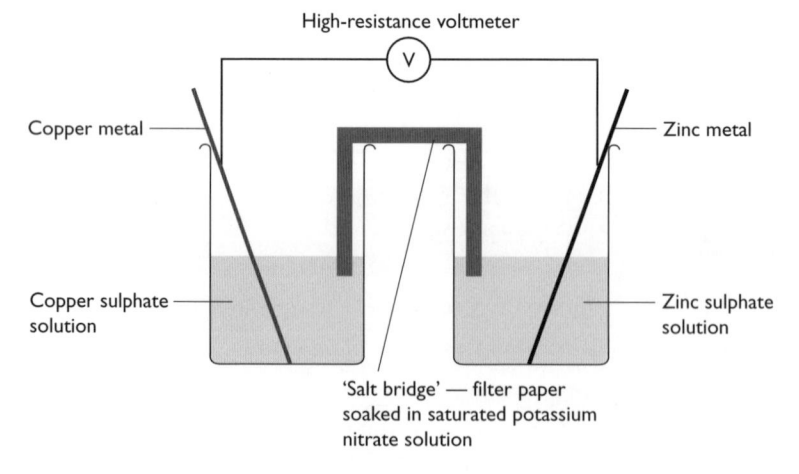

High-resistance voltmeter

Copper metal — Zinc metal

Copper sulphate solution — Zinc sulphate solution

'Salt bridge' — filter paper soaked in saturated potassium nitrate solution

The zinc metal will become negative because the reaction $Zn(s) \rightarrow Zn^{2+} + 2e^-$ will occur to a greater extent than $Cu(s) \rightarrow Cu^{2+} + 2e^-$.

Thus, the zinc rod is at a more negative potential than the copper rod. Electrons flow from the zinc to the copper in the external circuit. The voltmeter measures the potential difference between the two rods when very little current flows. Using $1.0 \, mol \, dm^{-3}$ solutions, the potential difference measured would be 1.1 V.

In order to measure the **electrode potential** of a half-cell, a standard electrode is needed. This is the hydrogen electrode. The cell needed to measure the **standard electrode potential** for a Zn/Zn²⁺ electrode is shown below:

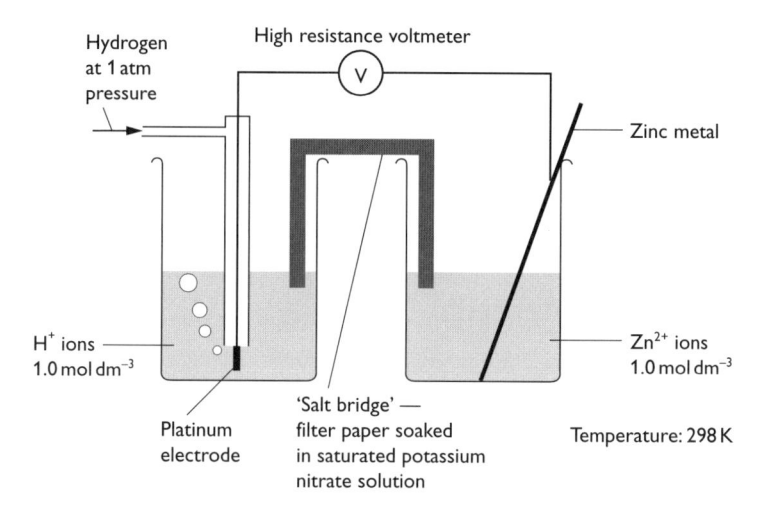

Note the *standard conditions*:
- Hydrogen at 1 atmosphere pressure
- Solution concentrations of 1.0 mol dm⁻³
- A temperature of 298 K

Tip All this detail needs to be learnt.

The zinc electrode in this cell is the negative one and the meter reads 0.76 V. Thus, we say that the standard electrode potential, $E^\ominus$, for the Zn/Zn²⁺ electrode is –0.76 V.

Redox reactions between two species in solution

There are some half-cells in which the metal electrode is not one of the reagents. These have a platinum electrode and the standard state is when the concentrations of the two species are equal. Some examples are shown below:

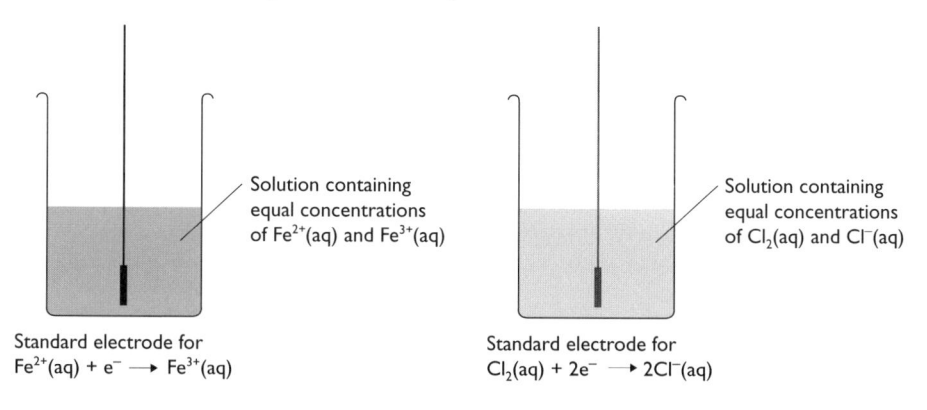

Standard electrode for
$Fe^{2+}(aq) + e^- \longrightarrow Fe^{3+}(aq)$

Standard electrode for
$Cl_2(aq) + 2e^- \longrightarrow 2Cl^-(aq)$

Some standard electrode potentials are given in the following table.

Half-cell	Half-equation	$E^{\ominus}/V$
$Zn^{2+}(aq)/Zn(s)$	$Zn^{2+}(aq) + 2e^- \longrightarrow Zn(s)$	−0.76
$Fe^{2+}(aq)/Fe(s)$	$Fe^{2+}(aq) + 2e^- \longrightarrow Fe(s)$	−0.44
$2H^+(aq)/H_2(g)$	$2H^+(aq) + 2e^- \longrightarrow H_2(g)$	0 (by definition)
$O_2(g)/OH^-(aq)$	$O_2(g) + 2H_2O(l) + 4e^- \longrightarrow 4OH^-(aq)$	+0.40
$I_2(aq)/2I^-(aq)$	$I_2(aq) + 2e^- \longrightarrow 2I^-(aq)$	+0.54
$Fe^{3+}(aq)/Fe^{2+}(aq)$	$Fe^{3+}(aq) + e^- \longrightarrow Fe^{2+}(aq)$	+0.77
$MnO_4^-(aq)/Mn^{2+}(aq)$	$MnO_4^-(aq) + 8H^+(aq) + 5e^- \longrightarrow Mn^{2+}(aq) + 4H_2O(l)$	+1.51

Use of electrode potentials

Calculating $E^{\ominus}_{cell}$

This is done by taking the difference (*including* sign) between the two standard electrode potentials. The half-cell that is higher up in the table is the negative terminal of the cell, but the value of $E^{\ominus}_{cell}$ is quoted as a number without sign. The units are V. For example, $E^{\ominus}_{cell}$ for a cell consisting of a $Zn^{2+}(aq)/Zn(s)$ electrode and an $Fe^{3+}(aq)/Fe^{2+}(aq)$ electrode is 0.77 − (−0.76), which equals 1.53 V.

Making predictions about reacting substances

To do this, it is often useful to draw an **electrode potential chart**. The one below uses the data from the table above.

$E^{\ominus}/V$	Half-equation
−0.76	$Zn^{2+}(aq) + 2e^- \longrightarrow Zn(s)$
−0.44	$Fe^{2+}(aq) + 2e^- \longrightarrow Fe(s)$
0	$2H^+(aq) + 2e^- \longrightarrow H_2(g)$
+0.40	$O_2(g) + 2H_2O(l) + 4e^- \longrightarrow 4OH^-(aq)$
+0.54	$I_2(aq) + 2e^- \longrightarrow 2I^-(aq)$
+0.77	$Fe^{3+}(aq) + e^- \longrightarrow Fe^{2+}(aq)$
+1.51	$MnO_4^-(aq) + 8H^+(aq) + 5e^- \longrightarrow Mn^{2+}(aq) + 4H_2O(l)$

Note that in the chart:
- the half-equations are always written with electrons on the left-hand side of the equation — therefore, the *oxidised form* (e.g. Zn^{2+} rather than Zn) is on the *left*
- the most negative electrode potentials are at the *top*
- the substance at the bottom-left is the best *oxidising agent* and the substance at the top-right is the best *reducing agent*
- when two electrodes are set up in a cell, *electrons will flow through the external circuit to the half-cell with the more positive electrode potential*

Tip Use the final bullet point to explain your predictions.

OCR *(Salters)* Unit 2849

Thus, if the $Zn^{2+}(aq)/Zn(s)$ and $I_2(aq)/2I^-(aq)$ half-cells are considered, the zinc one will supply electrons through the external circuit to the (more positive) iodine one. Therefore, the reactions that occur are:

$Zn(aq) \longrightarrow Zn^{2+}(s) + 2e^-$ (i.e. the *reverse* of what is printed above)
$I_2(aq) + 2e^- \longrightarrow 2I^-(aq)$

This shows that zinc metal will reduce iodine but zinc(II) ions will *not* oxidise iodide ions.

It can also be seen that zinc metal will react with any of the substances on the left-hand side of the half-equations below –0.76 V, i.e. Fe^{2+}, H^+, Fe^{3+} and MnO_4^-/H^+. However, I^- will only react with those substances on the left-hand side of half-equations below +0.54 V, i.e. MnO_4^-/H^+ and Fe^{3+}.

To write equations for reactions which are feasible
This follows on from the above. When a reaction between two reagents is predicted, we say that the reaction between them is *feasible*. It may not happen if the activation energy is too large and, consequently, the reaction is very slow.

The steps that are needed to write equations, using the chart, are as follows:
- Write down the *upper* half-equation *reversed* (i.e. electrons on the *right*).
- Copy the lower half-equation as it is written.
- Make equal the number of electrons transferred in each half-equation by suitable multiplication or division.
- Add the equations together (the number of electrons will then cancel).

Example 1
Zinc will react with Fe^{3+}. The half-equations are:
$Zn(s) \longrightarrow Zn^{2+}(aq) + 2e^-$ (upper half-equation reversed)
$2Fe^{3+}(aq) + 2e^- \longrightarrow 2Fe^{2+}(aq)$ (lower half-equation doubled to get $2e^-$)
Adding: $Zn(s) + 2Fe^{3+}(aq) \longrightarrow 2Fe^{2+}(aq) + Zn^{2+}(aq)$
(the numbers of electrons cancel out)

Example 2
Purple manganate(VII) is reduced in acid conditions by iodide ions, $I^-(aq)$. The half-equations are:
$10I^-(aq) \longrightarrow 5I_2(aq) + 10e^-$
(upper half-equation reversed and multiplied by 5 to get ten electrons)
$2MnO_4^-(aq) + 16H^+(aq) + 10e^- \longrightarrow 2Mn^{2+}(aq) + 8H_2O(l)$
(lower half-equation doubled to get ten electrons)
Adding: $2MnO_4^-(aq) + 10I^-(aq) + 16H^+(aq) \longrightarrow 2Mn^{2+}(aq) + 5I_2(aq) + 8H_2O(l)$

Rusting

This is an electrochemical process. The two half-equations are:
$Fe^{2+}(aq) + 2e^- \longrightarrow Fe(s)$ $E^\ominus = -0.44$ V
$O_2(g) + 2H_2O(l) + 4e^- \longrightarrow 4OH^-(aq)$ $E^\ominus = +0.40$ V

The overall equation is derived:
Equation 1: $Fe(s) \longrightarrow Fe^{2+}(aq) + 2e^-$ (upper half-equation reversed)
Equation 2: $\frac{1}{2}O_2(g) + H_2O(l) + 2e^- \longrightarrow 2OH^-(aq)$ (lower half-equation halved to get 2e⁻)
Adding: $\frac{1}{2}O_2(g) + H_2O(l) + Fe(s) \longrightarrow Fe^{2+}(aq) + 2OH^-(aq)$

The next reactions are:
$Fe^{2+}(aq) + 2OH^-(aq) \longrightarrow Fe(OH)_2$
$Fe(OH)_2$ is then oxidised by oxygen in the air to $Fe_2O_3.xH_2O$ (rust).

Equation 2 happens where there is *more* oxygen. Equation 1 (the corrosion of iron) happens where there is *less* oxygen — often at the bottom of a pit in the metal. This causes serious damage.

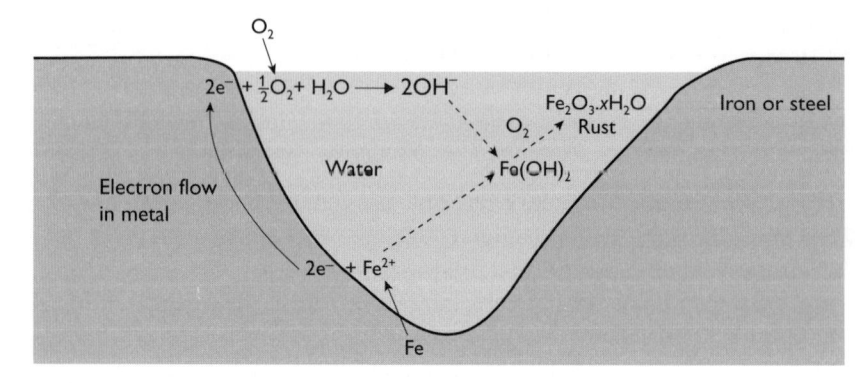

Tip It would be useful to learn this.

Analytical methods

Colorimetry

A colorimeter is used to measure the concentration of a coloured substance in a solution. It works by measuring the amount of light of a particular colour (determined by a coloured filter) that passes through the solution.

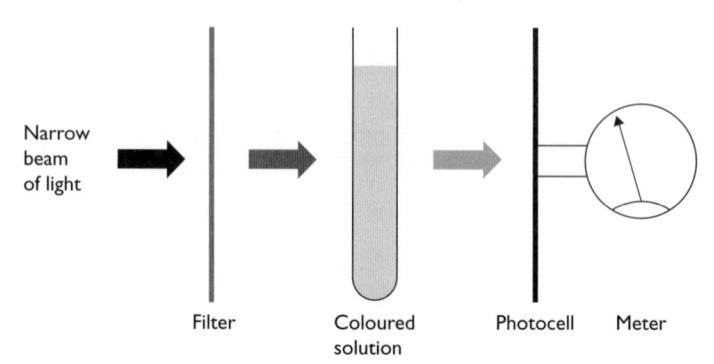

The colour of the filter is complementary to the colour of the solution. For example, a green filter is used for a purple solution, because purple solutions absorb green light and transmit purple light. The meter reads the **absorbance** (% light absorbed).

The best way to relate absorbance to concentration is to use a **calibration graph**.

The steps in measuring the concentration of a coloured solution with a colorimeter are as follows:
- Select a suitable filter.
- Adjust absorbance to zero, using a blank tube containing water.
- Make up several solutions of the coloured substance of *known concentration*.
- Find the absorbance for each of these concentrations.
- Plot a graph of concentration against absorbance. This is the calibration graph.
- Find the absorbance for the solution of unknown concentration.
- Read off the concentration of the unknown solution from the calibration graph.

Manganate(VII) titrations

Manganate(VII) titrations can be used to measure the concentration of a substance in aqueous solution if it reduces manganate(VII) ions in acid conditions. As you can see from the table on page 48, manganate(VII) is easily reduced, so it is suitable to titrate with many reducing agents.

The steps in carrying out such a titration are as follows:
- Fill a burette with a potassium manganate(VII) solution of *known concentration*.
- Add a *known volume* (measured by pipette) of substance X to a conical flask.
- Add an approximately equal volume of 1 mol dm^{-3} sulphuric acid to the flask.
- Titrate the solution of substance X with manganate(VII), while swirling the flask, until the *first permanent trace of pink colour* appears.
- Repeat until several titration results are within 0.1 cm^3 and calculate the mean value.

To calculate the concentration of substance X:
- Use half-equations to write the equation for the reaction of X with MnO_4^- (see page 49).
- Use your titration result and the known concentration of the manganate(VII) solution to work out the number of moles of manganate(VII) added.
- Use the equation to work out the number of moles of X in the flask.
- Use the known volume of X and the number of moles of X to work out the concentration of X.

Mass spectrometry

You meet this topic in **What's in a medicine?**

This tells us the M_r of the molecule and gives information about its structure from the fragments formed in the spectrometer.

A2 Chemistry

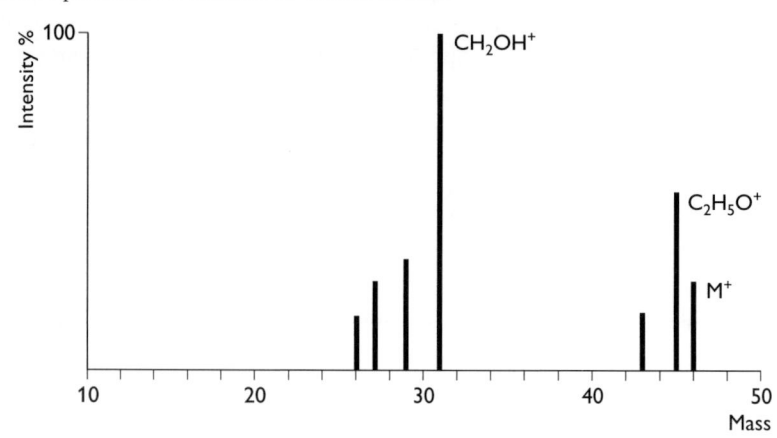

The mass spectrum of ethanol is shown below.

Note that all the peaks are caused by singly charged positive ions. You *must* show the + sign when identifying any peak. The peak of highest mass (called the molecular ion peak or M⁺) gives the M_r — here 46. The other peaks are fragments. A good way to begin analysing fragments is to look at the *masses lost*. A loss of 1 (45) indicates the loss of a single hydrogen, almost certainly the hydroxyl one. A loss of 15 (31) indicates loss of CH_3. Notice there is no peak at 15; this means that the methyl groups are formed as radicals rather than ions and are therefore not detected.

Infrared spectroscopy

You meet this topic in **What's in a medicine?**

Infrared spectroscopy identifies some of the functional groups found in molecules. The infrared spectrum of ethanol (liquid film) is shown below.

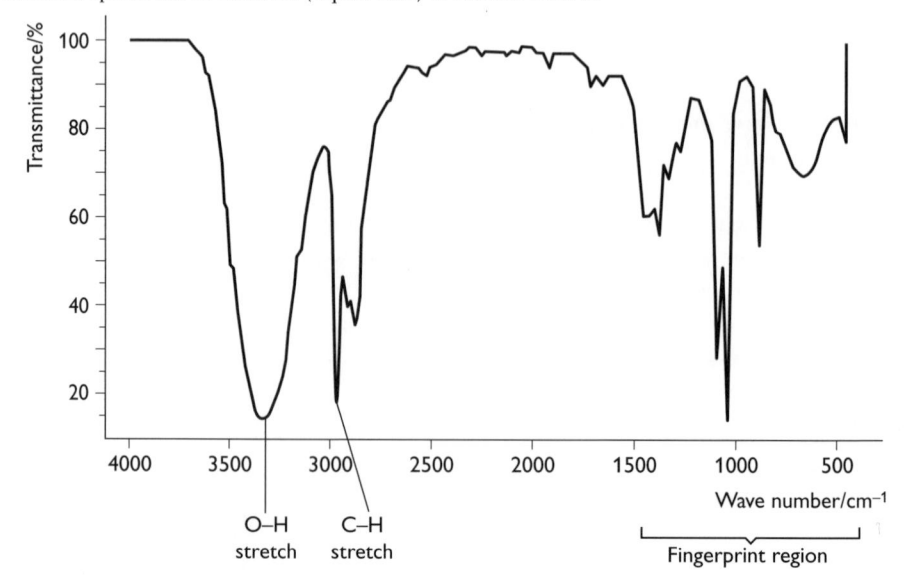

OCR*(Salters)* Unit 2849

The O–H and C–H stretches show up well. C–O is also present at 1050 cm⁻¹ but it is the 'fingerprint region' which is difficult to interpret, since other stretching (and bending) modes can get in the way. Usually, it is best to look at absorptions above 1500 cm⁻¹, which are much clearer. As well as the two stretches shown, always look out for C=O around 1700 cm⁻¹. The *Data Sheet* enables you to make a judgement about which type of C=O compound is present (e.g. aldehydes are usually in the range 1720–1740 cm⁻¹, while esters are in the range 1735–1750 cm⁻¹).

Tip Don't forget the units (cm⁻¹) when identifying peaks.

Nuclear magnetic resonance spectroscopy

You meet this topic in **Engineering proteins**. Nuclear magnetic resonance spectroscopy is sometimes called ¹H NMR or proton NMR to distinguish it from other types of NMR which deal with other nuclei. However, it is the only form of NMR you are expected to know about.

The sample is placed in a powerful magnetic field and a band of radio frequencies is applied as pulses to a coil round the sample. Different hydrogen atoms in different molecular environments absorb slightly different frequencies. These are described on the spectrum as **chemical shifts**, where the absorptions of the hydrogen atoms in tetramethylsilane (TMS), Si(CH₃)₄, are taken as the zero point.

Tip The detail in the above paragraph is useful background to help you understand what is going on, but you do *not* need to learn it.

The NMR spectrum shows the number of hydrogen atoms in different environments.

Example
Ethanol has the structure:

$$H-\underset{\underset{H}{|}}{\overset{\overset{H}{|}}{C}}-\underset{\underset{H}{|}}{\overset{\overset{H}{|}}{C}}-O-H$$

The NMR spectrum of ethanol is shown below:

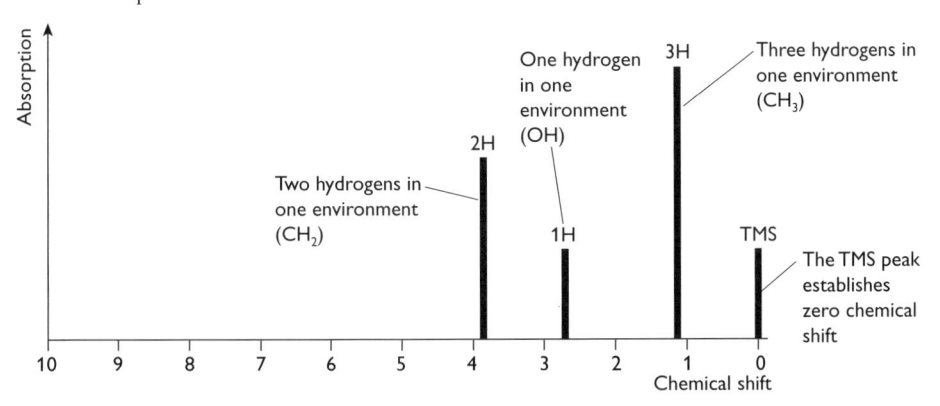

To analyse an NMR spectrum:
- Look first at the number of different hydrogen environments. For example, ethanol has three.
- Then look at the number of hydrogens in each environment. Ethanol has three in one environment, two in another and one in a third, as shown on the spectrum above. Much can be worked out from the number of environments and the number of hydrogen atoms in each.
- If necessary, use the *Data Sheet* to identify these. Remember that the values shown on the *Data Sheet* are only approximate.

Questions & Answers

A2 Chemistry

In this section of the guide, there are five questions which between them test every lettered statement in the specification. They represent the kinds of question you will get in the unit test, in that they start with a context and they contain a wide range of subject matter from the whole specification. Unlike in the real thing, there are no lines or spaces left for the answers. Instead, the presence of a space or number of lines is indicated. The number of marks is, of course, also shown. However, taken together, these questions are much longer than a single paper, so do not try to do them all in 90 minutes.

After each question, you will find the answers of two candidates — Candidate A and Candidate B (using different candidates for each question). In each case, Candidate A is performing at the C/D level, while Candidate B is an A-grade candidate.

Examiner's comments

All candidate responses are followed by examiner's comments. These are preceded by the icon *e* and indicate where credit is due. In the weaker answers, they also point out areas for improvement, specific problems and common errors.

How to use this section

- Do the question, giving yourself a time limit of a minute a mark; do not look at the candidates' answers or examiner's comments before you attempt the question yourself.
- Compare your answers with the candidates' answers and decide what the correct answer is; still do not look at the examiner's comments while doing this.
- Finally, look at the examiner's comments.

Completing this section will teach you a lot of chemistry and vastly improve your exam technique.

Question 1

Steel for a surgeon

A steel plant sets out to make stainless steel for surgeons' knives. The required specification of some important elements in the steel is given in the table, together with the specification of the blast furnace iron from which the steel is to be made.

Element	Steel/%	Blast furnace iron/%
Carbon	0.11	4.5
Silicon	0.35	0.60
Manganese	0.65	0.35
Chromium	12.5	trace
Phosphorus	0.03	0.10
Sulphur	0.01	0.5

(a) Sulphur is removed by reaction with magnesium. Write a balanced chemical equation for this reaction. *(space)* (1 mark)

(b) Describe the general effect of the percentage of carbon on the properties of a steel sample. *(3 lines)* (2 marks)

(c) The silicon content of the iron has to be reduced. The silicon is oxidised in the steel-making process.
  (i) How is the silicon oxidised? *(1 line)* (1 mark)
  (ii) The SiO_2 reacts with calcium oxide to form slag. Write a balanced chemical equation for this reaction. *(space)* (2 marks)

(d) Manganese is an element which has to be added at the end of the steel-making process.
  (i) Use your periodic table to complete the electronic structure of the Mn^{2+} ion.

  [↑↓] [↑↓] [↑↓][↑↓][↑↓] [↑↓] [↑↓][↑↓][↑↓] [ ][ ][ ][ ][ ] [ ]
   1s   2s   2p   3s   3p   3d   4s
  (2 marks)

  (ii) Explain, in terms of your answer to (i), why manganese is described as a transition metal. *(2 lines)* (2 marks)

(e) The manganese in steel is oxidised to the purple MnO_4^- ion, which can be used to determine the percentage of manganese in the steel.
  (i) Give the oxidation states of manganese in Mn^{2+} and MnO_4^-. *(1 line)* (2 marks)
  (ii) Give the *general property* of transition metals illustrated by part (i). *(1 line)* (1 mark)
  (iii) Explain this property in terms of electron energy levels. *(2 lines)* (2 marks)
  (iv) Explain, in terms of parts of the visible spectrum, why a MnO_4^- solution looks purple. *(3 lines)* (2 marks)
  (v) Describe how a colorimeter can be used to measure the concentration of a MnO_4^- solution which is known to be approximately $0.001\,mol\,dm^{-3}$. *(5 lines)* (6 marks)

In this question, 1 mark is available for quality of written communication.

57

question 1

(f) Potassium manganate(VII) titrations can be used to calculate the percentage of iron in substances such as iron tablets. In an experiment, an iron tablet of mass 1.60 g is dissolved in dilute sulphuric acid and the solution is made up to 250 cm³. 10.0 cm³ portions of the solution are titrated against 0.0100 mol dm⁻³ manganate(VII) solution. 21.1 cm³ are required.

  (i) Name the piece of apparatus that is used to:
   - make the solution up to 250 cm³ *(1 line)* (1 mark)
   - measure out 10.0 cm³ of solution *(1 line)* (1 mark)
  (ii) What would you see at the end-point of the titration? *(1 line)* (1 mark)
  (iii) Calculate the number of moles of manganate(VII) in 21.1 cm³ of 0.0100 mol dm⁻³ solution. *(space)* (1 mark)
  (iv) The iron tablet contains iron as Fe^{2+} ions. Five Fe^{2+} ions react with one manganate(VII) ion. Calculate the number of moles of iron present in the 250 cm³ solution, hence the mass of iron and hence the percentage of iron in the iron tablet. [A_r: Fe, 56] *(space)* (4 marks)
  (v) Excess aqueous sodium hydroxide is added to some of the iron tablet solution remaining after the titration. Say what would be seen and write an equation for the reaction. *(1 line, space)* (4 marks)

(g) The chromium in the steel can be identified by the complexes it forms. Two such complexes are shown in the equilibrium below:

$$[Cr(NH_3)_5Cl]^{2+}(aq) + NH_3(aq) \rightleftharpoons [Cr(NH_3)_6]^{3+}(aq) + Cl^-(aq)$$
  Complex A   Complex B

Complex A is purple and complex B is yellow.

  (i) Complex A has two ligands, one of which is charged. Give the formulae of the two ligands. *(1 line)* (2 marks)
  (ii) Draw a diagram to illustrate the shape of *complex A*. *(space)* (1 mark)
  (iii) Name the *type* of reaction in the equation above. *(1 line)* (1 mark)
  (iv) Write the equilibrium constant, K_c, for the equilibrium above in terms of [complex A], [NH_3], [complex B] and [Cl^-]. *(space)* (2 marks)
  (v) Give the units of this equilibrium constant (if any). *(1 line)* (1 mark)
  (vi) The numerical value of the equilibrium constant is 2.0 at a certain temperature. Use the data in the table below to calculate the concentration of *complex B* under these conditions. *(space)* (2 marks)

Substance	Concentration/mol dm⁻³
Complex A	0.100
Ammonia	0.050
Chloride ion	0.020

  (vii) Changing which *one* of the following would most affect the equilibrium constant of the reaction: temperature, pressure or concentration of ammonia? *(1 line)* (1 mark)
  (viii) Write the equilibrium expression associated with the stability constant of complex B. *(space)* (2 marks)

OCR (Salters) Unit 2849

(ix) Edta^{4-} is a polydentate ligand that forms a stable complex with chromium ions. Explain what polydentate means. *(2 lines)* (1 mark)

(h) (i) Iron scrap is added to the blast furnace iron before the steel is made. Give one reason for doing this. *(2 lines)* (1 mark)

(ii) Iron is used as a catalyst in the Haber process. Explain, in terms of their electronic structure, why transition metals make good catalysts for gas reactions. *(3 lines)* (3 marks)

Total: 52 marks

■ ■ ■

Candidates' answers to Question 1

Candidate A
(a) Mg + S + O ⟶ MgSO

Candidate B
(a) Mg + S ⟶ MgS

Candidate A is perhaps confused by the fact that an oxygen blow occurs later. In any case, his equation is wrong; oxygen should be O_2 and magnesium sulphate $MgSO_4$, so no marks are awarded. Candidate B has realised that this is a very simple first part and scores the mark.

Candidate A
(b) Large amounts of carbon make it brittle whereas small amounts make it bendy.

Candidate B
(b) High-carbon steel is hard, whereas low-carbon steel is called mild steel.

Candidate A has used rather simple language but he has scored both marks. Candidate B scores the first mark (though 'brittle' would be a better answer than 'hard'). However, the second part of her answer, while correct, does not answer the question and so does not score.

Candidate A
(c) (i) Silicon is already present as its oxide.

Candidate B
(c) (i) The oxygen blow oxidises it.

Candidate A has failed to realise that the whole point behind the BOS process is to oxidise the impurities! His answer is wrong and does not score whereas Candidate B is correct and gains the mark.

Candidate A
(c) (ii) $CaO_2 + SiO_2$ ⟶ $CaSiO_4$

Candidate B
(c) (ii) $CaO + SiO_2$ ⟶ $CaSiO_3$

A2 Chemistry

question 1

✏️ Candidate A scores 1 mark for a balanced equation but loses the second mark because the formulae of calcium oxide and calcium silicate are wrong. Candidate B's equation is correct and scores 2 marks. It is important to learn how to write simple formulae and get them right in exams!

Candidate A
(d) (i)

↑↓	↑↓	↑↓ ↑↓ ↑↓	↑↓	↑↓ ↑↓ ↑↓	↑ ↑ ↑		↑↓
1s	2s	2p	3s	3p	3d		4s

Candidate B
(d) (i)

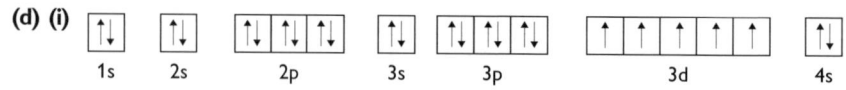

↑↓	↑↓	↑↓ ↑↓ ↑↓	↑↓	↑↓ ↑↓ ↑↓	↑ ↑ ↑ ↑ ↑	↑↓
1s	2s	2p	3s	3p	3d	4s

✏️ Neither candidate has done particularly well here! Candidate A has not appreciated that the two electrons manganese loses come from the 4s sub-shell. They may be first in but they are also first out! Candidate B has written the electron structure for the *atom*, not the *ion*. Both score 1 mark.

Candidate A
(d) (ii) It is in the *d*-block of the periodic table.

Candidate B
(d) (ii) Some of its *d* sub-shells are incomplete.

✏️ Candidate A's answer is wrong. Candidate B is nearer but still only scores 1 out of 2 marks because she does not say that *in some of its compounds* the d-subshell is incomplete.

Candidate A
(e) (i) +2; +8

Candidate B
(e) (i) +2; +7

✏️ Candidate B is correct and scores both marks. Candidate A has perhaps forgotten that the oxidation states of the atoms in an ion must add to the *charge on the ion* — in this case –1.

Candidate A
(e) (ii) They have different charges on their ions.

Candidate B
(e) (ii) They have variable oxidation states.

✏️ Candidate A is not quite right. The ion charges may vary, but it is the variation of oxidation state that is important. Candidate B is correct, for 1 mark.

Candidate A
(e) (iii) There are many different stable arrangements.

OCR (Salters) Unit 2849

Candidate B

(e) (iii) There are many possible stable arrangements of the 3*d* electrons.

e Candidate A has offered part of the answer and scores 1 mark. Candidate B has included the extra detail and gains the second mark.

Candidate A

(e) (iv) It absorbs in the green region, so it looks purple.

Candidate B

(e) (iv) It absorbs the complementary colour to purple.

e Both candidates have been rather vague and only score 1 mark out of 2 marks. The marks are for: *absorbs green (or complementary colour); transmits purple*. Thus, neither candidate has given sufficient detail to score the second mark.

Candidate A

(e) (v) Put tube of water into colorimeter and zero it. Then put in coloured tube. Read meter. Meter reading gives concentration.

Candidate B

(e) (v) Make up a series of solutions of manganate(VII) in the right range. Measure the colorimeter readings for each of these solutions and plot a calibration graph. Then take the reading for the unknown solution and read its concentration off the graph.

e There are 5 marks for content here. However, there are more than five marking points. Candidate A scores a mark for the idea of a reference tube. He then gains another mark for '…put in coloured tube…read meter', so he has 2 marks. He fails to score the quality of written communication mark because he has written in note form and also because he has not used technical terms (e.g. calibration) correctly. Candidate B scores 1 mark for 'in the right range' but she has not mentioned 'known concentrations', and so misses a mark. She scores 2 marks for her next sentence and 2 more for her last sentence, so on this generous mark scheme she gains 5 marks. She also earns the quality of written communication mark for logical sentences and correct use of the technical terms 'calibration graph' and 'concentration'. Both candidates would have been well advised to write 'absorbance' rather than 'readings'.

Candidate A

(f) (i) Measuring cylinder; burette

Candidate B

(f) (i) Standard flask; pipette

e Candidate A has forgotten his AS practical work! Measuring cylinders are not accurate enough for this type of use and while a burette could be used to measure 10 cm^3 of solution accurately, a chemist would always use a pipette. So, no marks here. Candidate B has named the right equipment and scores both marks. Note that a standard flask is sometimes called a graduated or volumetric flask.

question 1

Candidate A

(f) (ii) The indicator changes colour.

Candidate B

(f) (ii) A pale pink colour is visible.

e Candidate A has confused manganate(VII) and acid–base titrations. Manganate titrations are self-indicating and the colour change should be given. Candidate B only just scores the mark. The best answer is *first permanent trace of pink (or purple) colour*.

Candidate A

(f) (iii) $21.1 \times 0.01/1000 = 2.11 \times 10^{-4}$

Candidate B

(f) (iii) 2.11×10^{-4} mol

e Both candidates are correct, for 1 mark. Candidate B has given units — which is always a good idea — but because of the way the question is phrased, they are not essential here.

Candidate A

(f) (iv) Percentage of iron = $\dfrac{2.11 \times 10^{-4} \times 56 \times 100}{5 \times 1.60}$ = 0.15%

Candidate B

(f) (iv) Moles Fe in one $10\,\text{cm}^3$ pipette = $5 \times 2.11 \times 10^{-4}$ mol
Moles Fe in $250\,\text{cm}^3$ flask = $5 \times 25 \times 2.11 \times 10^{-4}$ mol
Mass Fe in $250\,\text{cm}^3$ flask = $56 \times 5 \times 25 \times 2.11 \times 10^{-4}$ mol = $1.4770\,\text{g}$

Percentage = $\dfrac{1.4770 \times 100}{1.60}$ = 92.313%

e Candidate A has tried to do the whole calculation at once. Since he has got it wrong, it is far more difficult for the examiner to unravel what he has done than it would be if he had set out the answer in the same way as Candidate B. Candidate B has the correct steps, each of which scores 1 mark. Candidate A does not score the first mark for the mole ratio because he has it upside down. He missed the factor of 25 scaling up from a pipette to the whole flask. However, he scores the third mark for multiplying by 56 to convert to grams and the last mark for working out the percentage correctly. Candidate B has fallen at the final hurdle and given the answer to a ridiculous number of significant figures. She loses the final mark because of this. Three significant figures (92.3%) would be the best answer since all the experimental data are given to three significant figures. However, two or four significant figures would have been acceptable.

Candidate A

(f) (v) A yellow precipitate
$FeSO_4 + 2NaOH \longrightarrow Fe(OH)_2 + Na_2SO_4$

OCR (Salters) Unit 2849

Candidate B

(f) (v) A dark green precipitate

$$Fe^{2+} + 2OH^- \longrightarrow Fe(OH)_2(s)$$

e Both candidates have made a good effort. Candidate A has the colour of the precipitate wrong but his equation is fine. He scores 3 marks. Candidate B has the correct colour and has given an ionic equation, which is a more sophisticated answer. She scores all 4 marks.

Candidate A

(g) (i) Ammonia and chlorine

Candidate B

(g) (i) NH_3; Cl^-

e Candidate A has not read the question properly, otherwise he would have written formulae and *not* names. However, his answer is acceptable for the first ligand (but wrong for the second). Even 'chloride' would not have scored, as the charge was needed. He scores 1 mark. Candidate B is correct, for 2 marks.

Candidate A

(g) (ii)

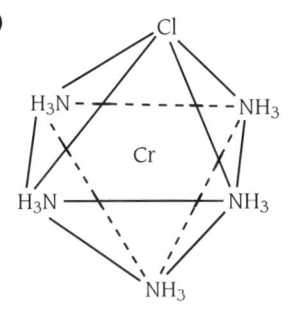

Candidate B

(g) (ii)

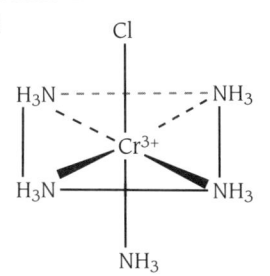

e Here are two rather different answers. However, both represent the structure correctly, so they each score the mark.

Candidate A

(g) (iii) Ligand exchange

A2 Chemistry

Candidate B

(g) (iii) Oxidation

e Candidate A is correct and scores the mark. There is no oxidation as the chromium remains in the +3 oxidation state throughout, so Candidate B does not score.

Candidate A

(g) (iv) $$K_c = \frac{[\text{complex A}] \times [\text{ammonia}]}{[\text{complex B}] \times [\text{chloride}]}$$

Candidate B

(g) (iv) $$K_c = \frac{[\text{complex B}] \times [\text{chloride}]}{[\text{complex A}] \times [\text{ammonia}]}$$

e Candidate A has the expression upside down. However, he still scores 1 out of 2 marks. Candidate B is correct, scoring both marks.

Candidate A

(g) (v) mol dm^{-3}

Candidate B

(g) (v) There are no units, since there are two concentrations on the top and two on the bottom.

e Candidate B is correct, for 1 mark. She has also given the reason, which was not asked for. Candidate A is wrong.

Candidate A

(g) (vi) [complex B] = 0.125 mol dm^{-3}

Candidate B

(g) (vi) $$[\text{complex B}] = \frac{K_c \times [\text{complex A}] \times [\text{ammonia}]}{[\text{chloride}]} = 0.50 \text{ mol dm}^{-3}$$

e Candidate A has shown no working, which is dangerous. However, the kind examiner has calculated the value which his expression in g(iv) would have given and he gains the 2 marks, as it is correct with 'error carried forward'. Candidate B is correct, scoring both marks.

Candidate A

(g) (vii) Concentration of ammonia

Candidate B

(g) (vii) Temperature

e Candidate A has presumably not realised that the question asks for the *effect on* the equilibrium constant and not the *position* of equilibrium. Changing the ammonia concentration will affect the position of equilibrium but not the equilibrium constant. Be careful here! Candidate B has the correct answer, for 1 mark.

Candidate A

(g) (viii) $[Cr(NH_3)_5Cl]^{2+}(aq) + NH_3(aq) \rightleftharpoons [Cr(NH_3)_6]^{3+}(aq) + Cl^-(aq)$

Candidate B

(g) (viii) $[Cr(NH_3)_6]^{3+}(aq) + 6H_2O(aq) \rightleftharpoons [Cr(H_2O)_6]^{3+}(aq) + 6NH_3(aq)$

🅔 Candidate A does not understand that stability constants for complexes are always measured relative to the complex with water, so he does not score, as he has simply copied out the equation in the question. Candidate B does better, but she has the equilibrium the wrong way round and so scores 1 out of 2 marks.

Candidate A

(g) (ix) It has lots of teeth.

Candidate B

(g) (ix) It has many (six) points of attachment to the central ion.

🅔 Candidate A has used the phrase he has learnt to remember the meaning of polydentate. To score, he had to interpret what 'teeth' are. Candidate B does this and gains the mark.

Candidate A

(h) (i) To achieve the right temperature.

Candidate B

(h) (i) To help with the recycling of iron.

🅔 Both are correct, for 1 mark. Candidate A's is a more sophisticated answer, but Candidate B's is equally acceptable.

Candidate A

(h) (ii) Catalysts speed up chemical reactions but are unchanged at the end. Iron does this well because of its incomplete *d* sub-shell.

Candidate B

(h) (ii) Transition metals have unfilled *d* orbitals. This enables gas molecules to be adsorbed (chemically bonded) to the surface, where reactions can occur more easily.

🅔 Candidate A starts very vaguely but scores 1 mark for mentioning the incomplete *d* sub-shell. Candidate B also mentions this, using different but equally acceptable terminology. Her next sentence scores the second mark. However, the last phrase is just too vague to score. Some mention of lowering the activation energy is needed for the final marking point. Candidate B scores 2 out of 3 marks.

The enzyme urease

The enzyme *urease* is present in many simple organisms. It catalyses the hydrolysis of toxic urea into ammonia and carbon dioxide.

$$O=C(NH_2)_2 + H_2O \rightarrow CO_2 + 2NH_3$$

The rate of this reaction can be followed in the laboratory by measuring the amount of alkaline ammonia produced.

(a) Suggest a method of measuring the amount of ammonia produced. *(3 lines)* (2 marks)

(b) Some data for the laboratory reactions of urease are given in the table below:

Experiment	Enzyme concentration/ mol dm^{-3}	Urea concentration/ mol dm^{-3}	Reaction rate/ mol dm^{-3} s^{-1}
A	1.0×10^{-5}	0.01	1.0×10^{-5}
B	2.0×10^{-5}	0.01	2.0×10^{-5}
C	1.0×10^{-5}	0.02	2.0×10^{-5}
D	1.0×10^{-5}	0.10	5.0×10^{-5}
E	1.0×10^{-5}	0.20	5.0×10^{-5}

(i) Use the results of experiments A, B and C to determine (at low substrate concentration) the orders of reaction with respect to enzyme concentration, [E], and substrate concentration, [S]. *(2 lines)* (2 marks)

(ii) Write a rate equation in terms of [E] and [S]. *(1 line)* (2 marks)

(iii) Write down the overall order of the reaction. *(1 line)* (1 mark)

(iv) Give the units of the rate constant for your rate equation. *(space)* (2 marks)

(v) Use the results of experiments D and E to work out the order of reaction with respect to substrate at high substrate concentration. Explain how you arrived at your answer. *(3 lines)* (2 marks)

(vi) Sketch the shape of the graph you would expect for substrate concentration (y-axis) against time (x-axis) when the reaction has the order, with respect to substrate, you determined in part (i). Mark two successive half-lives on your sketch. *(space)* (3 marks)

(c) Some students tried using compound A as a substrate for urease. No reaction occurred.

$$O=C(CH_3)(NH_2)$$

Compound A

OCR *(Salters)* Unit 2849

(i) Name the functional group in compound A. *(1 line)* (1 mark)
(ii) Write the equation for the hydrolysis of compound A with water, which occurs very slowly. *(space)* (2 marks)
(iii) Suggest, in terms of enzyme structure, why urease does not catalyse the hydrolysis of compound A. *(5 lines)* (4 marks)
(iv) Explain, in terms of enzyme structure, what is meant by an *enzyme inhibitor*. *(3 lines)* (2 marks)
(v) Describe another condition (other than the use of inhibitors) that stops an enzyme working, and describe how it does this. *(3 lines)* (3 marks)
(vi) Give *one* use of enzymes in industry. *(1 line)* (1 mark)
(d) Some students hydrolysed a sample of urease. Glycine and serine were among the amino acids in the product.

$$H_2N-\underset{\underset{H}{|}}{\overset{\overset{H}{|}}{C}}-COOH \qquad H_2N-\underset{\underset{H}{|}}{\overset{\overset{CH_2OH}{|}}{C}}-COOH$$

Glycine   Serine

(i) Suggest a technique that could have been used to separate the amino acids prior to identification. *(1 line)* (1 mark)
(ii) Draw the structure of the zwitterion that glycine forms in solution. *(space)* (2 marks)
(iii) Draw the structure of a dipeptide formed between a molecule of glycine and a molecule of serine. *(space)* (2 marks)
(iv) What *type* of reaction occurs when the molecule in part (iii) is formed from the two amino acids? *(1 line)* (1 mark)
(v) What name is given to the link between the two amino acids? *(1 line)* (1 mark)
(vi) One of the two amino acids is *chiral*. Draw diagrams of the three-dimensional structures of the two stereoisomers that result from this property, showing how they are related. *(space)* (3 marks)
(e) (i) There are three levels of protein structure. Briefly describe each.
 • Primary *(2 lines)* (1 mark)
 • Secondary *(2 lines)* (1 mark)
 • Tertiary *(2 lines)* (1 mark)
(ii) Explain why the primary structure of a protein is important in the function of the protein. *(2 lines)* (2 marks)
(iii) Give *two* interactions between chains that hold in shape the tertiary structure of a protein. *(2 lines)* (2 marks)
(iv) Give *one* other function of proteins in our bodies, apart from acting as enzymes. *(1 line)* (1 mark)

Total: 45 marks

Candidates' answers to Question 2

Candidate A
(a) Titrate with acid.

Candidate B
(a) Titrate with acid of known concentration.

e Candidate A scores 1 mark. Candidate B scores 2 because of the extra vital detail.

Candidate A
(b) (i) First

Candidate B
(b) (i) First; first

e Candidate A has not written down 'first' twice, so she does not score the second mark. Candidate B gains both marks.

Candidate A
(b) (ii) $k[E][S]$

Candidate B
(b) (ii) Rate = $k[E][S]$

e Candidate A has not written the complete rate equation (see Candidate B's answer) and scores 1 out of 2 marks. Candidate B gains both marks.

Candidate A
(b) (iii) First

Candidate B
(b) (iii) Second

e The answer is second-order (first + first). Candidate B gains the mark; Candidate A does not.

Candidate A
(b) (iv) $mol\ dm^{-3}\ s^{-1}$

Candidate B
(b) (iv) $k = \dfrac{rate}{[E][S]}$

Units = $\dfrac{mol\ dm^{-3}\ s^{-1}}{mol\ dm^{-3} \times mol\ dm^{-3}} = dm^3\ mol^{-1}\ s^{-1}$

e Since part (iv) follows on from part (iii), Candidate A is bound to have some difficulty getting it right and she has failed, though she has made a good effort. Candidate B scores both marks for a full answer that explains what he is doing.

OCR (Salters) Unit 2849

Candidate A

(b) (v) Zero, since it does not change with concentration.

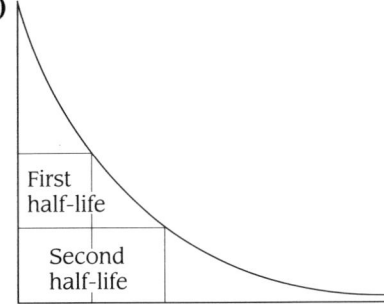

Candidate B

(b) (v) Zero, since the rate does not change when the concentration increases.

e Candidate A has the correct order for the reaction, for 1 mark, but loses the mark for the reason. It is the rate (not the order, as implied) that does not change with concentration. Candidate B is correct and scores 2 marks.

Candidate A
(b) (vi)

[Graph showing decay curve with "First half-life" and "Second half-life" marked]

Candidate B
(b) (vi) [S]

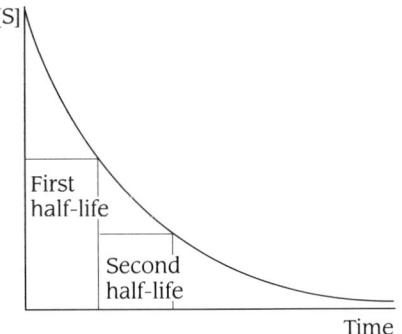

[Graph showing decay curve with [S] on y-axis and Time on x-axis, with "First half-life" and "Second half-life" marked]

e Both candidates score well. Candidate A has not marked the second half-life correctly but she has the correct shape for the curve. She has not labelled the axes, which is risky, though in this case there are no marks available for these labels because of the way the question is worded. She scores 2 marks. Candidate B's answer is completely correct, for 3 marks.

Candidate A
(c) (i) Amine

Candidate B
(c) (i) Amide

question 2

e Candidate A has made a very common error by confusing amines with amides. Learn functional groups *carefully*. (Here, remembering that *polyamides* exist might help.) Candidate B is correct, for 1 mark.

Candidate A

(c) (ii)

$$O=C\binom{CH_3}{NH_2} + H_2O \longrightarrow CO_2 + NH_3 + CH_4$$

Candidate B

(c) (ii) $CH_3CONH_2 + H_2O \longrightarrow CH_3COOH + NH_3$

e Candidate A has not recalled the hydrolysis of amides and therefore invented an equation based on the hydrolysis of urea. It is not right, but it scores 1 mark for ammonia as one of the products. Candidate B scores both marks for the correct equation.

Candidate A

(c) (iii) The enzyme is the lock, the substrate is the key. Compound A does not fit the lock.

Candidate B

(c) (iii) The enzyme has an active site (a cleft in the molecule) to which the urea binds by weak intermolecular forces. CH_3CONH_2 will not fit into this site, emphasising the importance of two NH_2 groups in the binding.

e Candidate A's answer is far too simplistic. However, she scores 2 marks for the idea of the substrate fitting and compound A not fitting. Candidate B has given a very good answer, for full marks.

Candidate A

(c) (iv) An inhibitor binds irreversibly onto the enzyme's active site.

Candidate B

(c) (iv) An inhibitor binds onto the enzyme's active site, stopping substrate molecules from getting there.

e Candidate A scores 1 mark for the idea of binding to the active site. Note that only some inhibitors bind irreversibly. However, with only 2 marks available, this would not be penalised. Candidate B has made the important point that the substrate is excluded and scores both marks.

Candidate A

(c) (v) pH change breaks the hydrogen bonds which hold the tertiary structure and the active site in shape.

Candidate B

(c) (v) Heating above a certain temperature breaks the hydrogen bonds holding the tertiary structure, and hence the active site, in shape.

OCR (Salters) Unit 2849

e Candidate A scores 2 out of 3 marks. She names a correct condition and says how denaturation works. However, changes in pH do not have much effect on hydrogen bonds — they affect ionic interactions — so she loses the third mark. Candidate B gives the correct cause of denaturation at high temperature.

Candidate A
(c) (vi) Brewing

Candidate B
(c) (vi) Cheese making

e Both candidates are correct, for 1 mark.

Candidate A
(d) (i) Hydrolysis

Candidate B
(d) (i) Chromatography

e Candidate A has not read the stem of the question correctly — the protein has already been hydrolysed. The correct answer is chromatography. Candidate B gains the mark.

Candidate A
(d) (ii)

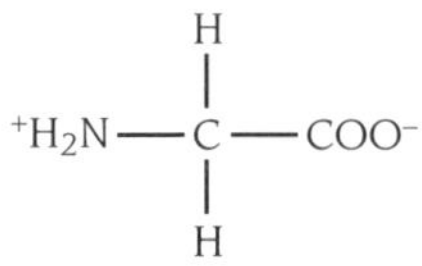

$$^+H_2N-\underset{\underset{H}{|}}{\overset{\overset{H}{|}}{C}}-COO^-$$

Candidate B
(d) (ii)

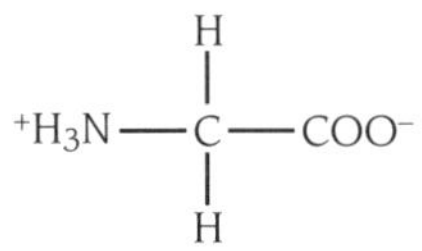

$$^+H_3N-\underset{\underset{H}{|}}{\overset{\overset{H}{|}}{C}}-COO^-$$

e Candidate A scores 1 mark only, as she has not realised that the NH_2 becomes NH_3^+ in forming the zwitterion. Candidate B scores both marks.

Candidate A
(d) (iii)

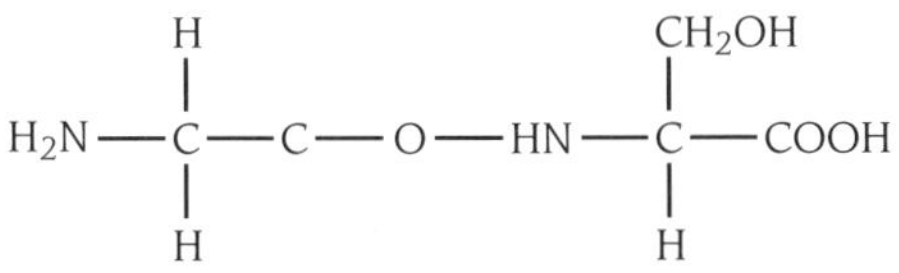

$$H_2N-\underset{\underset{H}{|}}{\overset{\overset{H}{|}}{C}}-C-O-HN-\underset{\underset{H}{|}}{\overset{\overset{CH_2OH}{|}}{C}}-COOH$$

Candidate B
(d) (iii)

$$H_2N-\underset{\underset{H}{|}}{\overset{\overset{H}{|}}{C}}-\overset{\overset{O}{||}}{C}-\overset{\overset{H}{|}}{N}-\underset{\underset{H}{|}}{\overset{\overset{CH_2OH}{|}}{C}}-COOH$$

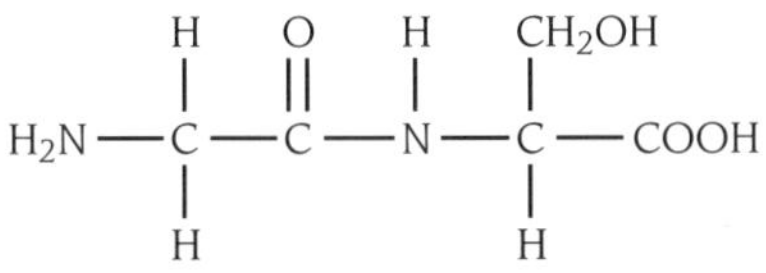

A2 Chemistry

question 2

🅔 Candidate A shows that she understands that a reaction occurs between NH_2 and COOH and scores 1 mark. However, the nature of the bond is wrong, as Candidate B's correct answer shows. He scores both marks.

Candidate A
(d) (iv) Elimination

Candidate B
(d) (iv) Condensation

🅔 Although water *is* eliminated, this type of reaction is condensation. Candidate A does not score. Candidate B gains the mark.

Candidate A
(d) (v) Amide

Candidate B
(d) (v) Peptide

🅔 Both candidates are correct, for 1 mark. These bonds can be called either (secondary) amide or peptide bonds.

Candidate A
(d) (vi)

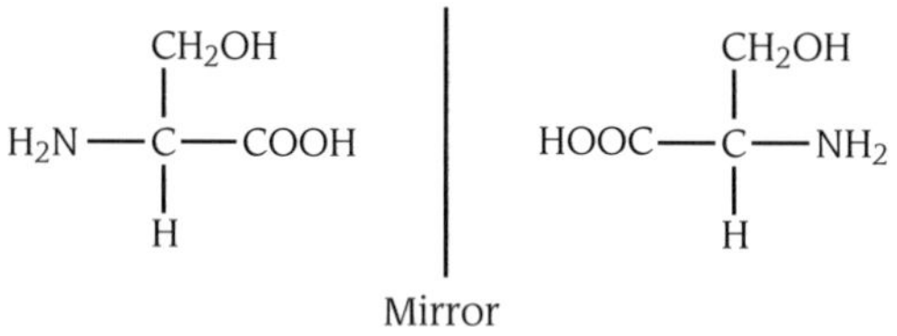

$$H_2N-\underset{\underset{H}{|}}{\overset{\overset{CH_2OH}{|}}{C}}-COOH \qquad HOOC-\underset{\underset{H}{|}}{\overset{\overset{CH_2OH}{|}}{C}}-NH_2$$

Mirror

Candidate B
(d) (vi)

[3-D wedge/dash structures of the two enantiomers with CH_2OH up, H back, and H_2N/COOH on wedges, mirror images]

Mirror

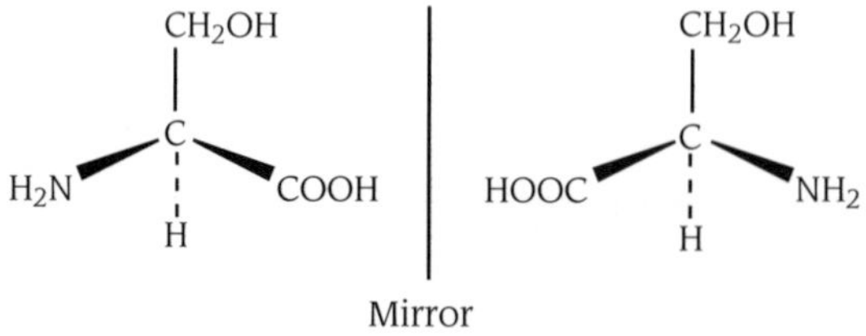

🅔 Candidate A has shown how the two enantiomers are related (object and mirror image) and made it clear that it is the arrangement of groups about the central carbon which is important, so she scores 2 marks. However, she has not drawn three-dimensional structures, as requested in the question. Candidate B has done this and scores all 3 marks.

Candidate A
(e) (i) Primary is the chain. Secondary is how the chain folds. Tertiary is how the folded chain is twisted, held together by intermolecular forces between R groups.

OCR(Salters) Unit 2849

Candidate B

(e) (i) Primary is the sequence of amino acids. Secondary is held together by hydrogen bonds. Tertiary is how the chain is twisted up.

e Candidate A scores all 3 marks. Her last phrase is not strictly necessary. Candidate B's answer scores 1 mark for the primary structure but then is too vague to score further marks.

Candidate A

(e) (ii) The sequence of amino acids determines how the protein folds, which determines what it does.

Candidate B

(e) (ii) It controls how it folds up, which dictates whether, for instance, it can act as an enzyme.

e Both candidates have given sufficient information to score 2 marks.

Candidate A

(e) (iii) Hydrogen and dipole

Candidate B

(e) (iii) Ionic interactions and covalent bonds

e Candidate A has been too brief and fails to score either mark. The interactions must be described as hydrogen *bonds* and *permanent dipole–permanent dipole forces*. Candidate B has chosen two different interactions, named them completely, and therefore scores 2 marks.

Candidate A

(e) (iv) Hair

Candidate B

(e) (iv) Structural

e Candidate A has been too specific and does not score. Candidate B has named a general function and gains the mark.

Question 3

A biodegradable plastic

'PHB' is a natural polyester made by certain bacteria. They use it as a reserve food supply. Plastic articles made from PHB are biodegradable. The structures of PHB and its monomer are:

(PHB structure: –(O–CH(CH₃)–CH₂–C(=O))– with the ester O–C(=O) group tinted)

(PHB monomer: H–O–CH(CH₃)–CH₂–C(=O)–O–H)

(a) (i) Name the functional group which is tinted in the structure of PHB. *(1 line)* (1 mark)

(ii) Give the systematic name of the PHB monomer. *(1 line)* (2 marks)

(iii) Suggest conditions for the hydrolysis of PHB to its monomer in the laboratory. *(2 lines)* (2 marks)

(iv) What technique would be used to purify a sample of the solid monomer made in this way? *(1 line)* (1 mark)

(v) Suggest conditions for the synthesis of PHB from its monomer in the laboratory. *(2 lines)* (2 marks)

(vi) Draw the structural formula of the salt formed when the PHB monomer reacts with sodium hydroxide. *(space)* (2 marks)

(vii) Give the number of peaks and their relative sizes that you would expect in the proton NMR spectrum of the PHB monomer. Explain your answer. *(4 lines)* (4 marks)

(b) Nylon Y could be made from the monomer X shown below:

(Monomer X: H₂N–CH(CH₃)–CH₂–C(=O)–OH, with the –C(=O)–OH group circled)

(i) Name the functional group circled in monomer X. *(1 line)* (1 mark)

(ii) Name the compound $C_2H_5NH_2$ which contains this functional group. *(1 line)* (1 mark)

(iii) Draw the structure of the repeating unit of nylon Y. *(space)* (2 marks)

(c) Another nylon is made by reacting the two monomers shown below:

(Cl–C(=O)–(CH₂)₄–C(=O)–Cl, with the right-hand –C(=O)–Cl circled; and H₂N–(CH₂)₆–NH₂)

(i) Name the functional group that is circled in the left-hand structure. *(1 line)* (1 mark)

(ii) Why is this functional group, rather than a carboxylic acid group, sometimes used for laboratory synthesis of nylon? *(2 lines)* (1 mark)

(iii) Name the small molecule that would be produced when the two monomers react. *(1 line)* (1 mark)

OCR *(Salters)* Unit 2849

(iv) Nylon was designed on purpose rather than being discovered by accident. Which naturally occurring polymers were the inspiration for its design?
(1 line) (1 mark)
(d) This part of the question compares the properties of **PHB** with those of nylon **Y**.
(i) Name the strongest type of intermolecular force found between the chains of:
- **PHB** *(1 line)* (1 mark)
- **nylon Y** *(1 line)* (1 mark)
(ii) A sample of nylon **Y** and a sample of **PHB** of the same shape and chain length are prepared. Which would you expect to:
- be less flexible?
- have the higher melting temperature?
Give reasons for your answers. *(4 lines)* (4 marks)
(iii) Suggest which of the two polymers would be more useful for making a carrier bag, giving your reasons. *(2 lines)* (1 mark)
(iv) Describe one *physical* change that can be made to a sample of nylon which will change its properties. *(2 lines)* (2 marks)
(e) Explain why biodegradable polymers are desirable. *(2 lines)* (2 marks)
(f) The ability to make **PHB** is coded in the **DNA** of a bacterial cell nucleus. The relevant genes can be placed in the nuclei of cells of plants such as cotton, which will then make **PHB**.
(i) Using symbols labelled 'base', 'sugar' and 'phosphate', draw the structure of the double chain of **DNA**. *(space)* (3 marks)
(ii) Name the intermolecular forces that link the two chains. *(1 line)* (1 mark)
(iii) Which part of **DNA** carries the code for a single amino acid in a protein? *(2 lines)* (2 marks)
(iv) Explain, in outline, how genes for synthesising **PHB** can be moved from bacterial cells to cotton plant cells. *(5 lines)* (3 marks)
(v) Give *one* advantage and *one* disadvantage of genetic engineering. *(4 lines)* (2 marks)

Total: 44 marks

■ ■ ■

Candidates' answers to Question 3

Candidate A
(a) (i) Carbonyl

Candidate B
(a) (i) Ester

🖉 Candidate A has not looked at the whole group. C=O is carbonyl on its own, but here it is part of an ester group. Candidate B is correct, for 1 mark.

Candidate A
(a) (ii) 2-hydroxybutanoic acid

Candidate B
(a) (ii) 3-hydroxybutanoic acid

question 3

A2 Chemistry

e Candidate A is almost correct and scores 1 mark. Candidate B has remembered that numbering in a carboxylic acid starts from the COOH carbon. She scores both marks.

Candidate A
(a) (iii) Reflux with concentrated sulphuric acid.

Candidate B
(a) (iii) Reflux with concentrated hydrochloric acid.

e Candidate A's conditions are harsh and the polymer would probably be dehydrated and turn brown. He scores 1 mark for heating. Candidate B's concentrated hydrochloric acid is also rather harsh but is just acceptable. She gains 2 marks. Moderately concentrated hydrochloric acid is the best reagent.

Candidate A
(a) (iv) Melting point

Candidate B
(a) (iv) Recrystallisation

e Candidate B is correct, for 1 mark. Taking a melting point is a test for purity but it does not purify a solid, so Candidate A does not score.

Candidate A
(a) (v) Heat with methanol and concentrated sulphuric acid.

Candidate B
(a) (v) Heat with concentrated sulphuric acid.

e Methanol is not required. Candidate A has not realised that the monomer has both the alcohol and the acid groups required to react with itself. Just concentrated sulphuric acid and heat are needed. He scores 1 mark only (for heating), since the mention of methanol contradicts the sulphuric acid mark. Candidate B scores 2 marks.

Candidate A
(a) (vi)

$$H-O-CH(CH_3)-CH_2-C(=O)-O-Na$$

Candidate B
(a) (vi)

$$H-O-CH(CH_3)-CH_2-C(=O)-O^-$$

e Candidate A scores 1 mark. He has the right idea but has not realised that the salt is ionic. Candidate B also only gains 1 mark, as she has not shown the sodium ion.

Candidate A
(a) (vii) 2 for OH; 3 for $CHCH_2$; 3 for CH_3

OCR (Salters) Unit 2849

Candidate B
(a) (vii) Size 1 for OH; size 1 for COOH; size 1 for CH; size 2 for CH$_2$; size 3 for CH$_3$

e Candidate A scores 1 mark for realising that hydrogen environments are involved. However, he then mixes up different environments and does not score further marks. Candidate B scores all 4 marks for getting all the environments and peak sizes correct.

Candidate A
(b) (i) Amino

Candidate B
(b) (i) Amine

e Both candidates are correct, for 1 mark. There are two alternative names.

Candidate A
(b) (ii) Ethamine

Candidate B
(b) (ii) Ethylamine

e Candidate A has made an attempt at the name, but it is not good enough to score. Candidate B is correct, for 1 mark.

Candidate A
(b) (iii)

$$H-\underset{\underset{H}{|}}{N}-\underset{\underset{CH_3}{|}}{CH}-CH_2-\underset{\overset{O}{\|}}{C}-\underset{\underset{H}{|}}{N}-\underset{\underset{CH_3}{|}}{CH}-CH_2-\underset{\overset{O}{\|}}{C}-H$$

Candidate B
(b) (iii)

$$-\underset{\underset{H}{|}}{N}-\underset{\underset{CH_3}{|}}{CH}-CH_2-\underset{\overset{O}{\|}}{C}-$$

e Candidate A has the right idea and scores 1 mark. However, he has not answered the question — he has given the result of condensing two monomers together, rather than giving the repeating unit when several combine together to form the polymer. Candidate B scores both marks.

Candidate A
(c) (i) Ethanoyl chloride

Candidate B
(c) (i) Acyl chloride

e Candidate A has given the name of one specific acyl chloride and does not score. Note how important it is to learn the names of functional groups in this unit! Candidate B is correct, for 1 mark.

Candidate A
(c) (ii) It is cheaper.

question 3

A2 Chemistry

Candidate B

(c) (ii) It reacts much faster.

e Candidate A has gone for quite a common answer. Even if it were correct, it should be qualified with a reason. However, he is wrong, as such chlorine-containing compounds are more expensive. Candidate B is correct, for 1 mark.

Candidate A

(c) (iii) Hydrochloric acid

Candidate B

(c) (iii) Hydrogen chloride

e Candidate A misses the mark by a whisker. Hydrochloric acid is not a small molecule; it is a solution containing ions. Thus, it does not score the mark. Hydrogen chloride is the correct answer, given by Candidate B, who scores 1 mark.

Candidate A

(c) (iv) Polyamides

Candidate B

(c) (iv) Proteins

e Candidate A has given another name which describes nylon, which does not score. Carothers based his design on proteins, so Candidate B is once again correct, for 1 mark.

Candidate A

(d) (i) Both have hydrogen bonding; however, there is more in nylon.

Candidate B

(d) (i) Permanent dipole–permanent dipole forces in PHB and hydrogen bonds in nylon

e Candidate A scores 1 mark for naming the strongest intermolecular force in nylon correctly. In PHB, the forces are permanent dipole–permanent dipole, since there are no –OH groups. Candidate B is correct, scoring both marks.

Candidate A

(d) (ii) Nylon would be less flexible and have the higher melting point because it has more hydrogen bonds.

Candidate B

(d) (ii) Nylon has stronger intermolecular forces, so it is less flexible. It also means that more energy is needed to separate the chains, so its melting temperature is higher.

e Candidate A should realise that a short answer like this is unlikely to gain 4 marks. He scores 1 mark for identifying nylon as being less flexible and having the higher melting

OCR (Salters) Unit 2849

point, and 1 mark for explaining this in terms of intermolecular forces. Candidate B scores 3 marks. She left out the crucial step of explaining low flexibility — *the chains cannot move over each other easily.*

Candidate A

(d) (iii) Nylon, as it is stronger (it has more hydrogen bonds).

Candidate B

(d) (iii) PHB, as it is more flexible.

☑ There is no definite answer here. Both candidates have made valid points and score the mark. In a 50/50 situation, there can be no mark for the choice of polymer alone, so the reason is vital.

Candidate A

(d) (iv) It will change if it is heated above its glass temperature.

Candidate B

(d) (iv) Nylon can be 'cold-drawn', that is, it can be gradually stretched to create more crystalline regions which make it have a higher tensile strength.

☑ Candidate A should realise that nylon, being flexible, is above its glass temperature already, so he does not score. Candidate B gives the expected answer and scores both marks, one for saying what is done and one for the resulting change in property.

Candidate A

(e) They can be broken down when buried in the ground.

Candidate B

(e) They can be broken down quickly by bacteria, thus avoiding the pollution caused by most plastics, which take years to break down.

☑ Candidate A scores 1 of the 2 marks but has not explained fully why breaking them down is desirable. Candidate B has done this and scores 2 marks.

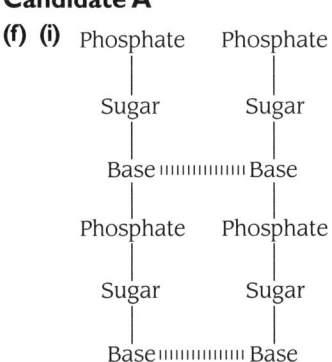

Candidate A

(f) (i)
```
Phosphate      Phosphate
    |              |
  Sugar          Sugar
    |              |
   Base ⅲⅲⅲⅲ Base
    |              |
Phosphate      Phosphate
    |              |
  Sugar          Sugar
    |              |
   Base ⅲⅲⅲⅲ Base
```

question 3

Candidate B

(f) (i)

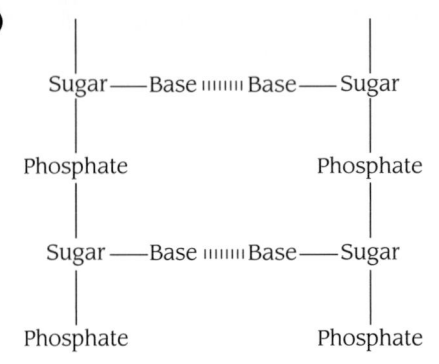

```
    |                    |
Sugar──Base ⋯⋯ Base──Sugar
    |                    |
Phosphate            Phosphate
    |                    |
Sugar──Base ⋯⋯ Base──Sugar
    |                    |
Phosphate            Phosphate
```

e Candidate A is confused. He understands that the two chains are linked through the bases and so scores 1 mark for this. However, he loses the other 2 marks by putting the bases in the chain, instead of sticking out from the sugars. Candidate B gains full marks.

Candidate A

(f) (ii) Weak intermolecular forces

Candidate B

(f) (ii) Hydrogen bonds

e Candidate B is correct, for 1 mark. Candidate A's answer is too vague.

Candidate A

(f) (iii) The bases

Candidate B

(f) (iii) A set of three adjacent bases

e Candidate A scores 1 mark for knowing it is something to do with the bases. Candidate B scores the second mark for knowing that the code is three bases.

Candidate A

(f) (iv) The genes can be cut from the bacteria and placed in the plant cells.

Candidate B

(f) (iv) Enzymes are used to cut the genes (section of DNA) from the bacterial DNA. Other enzymes are used to cut the cotton plant's DNA. The PHB gene is spliced into the cotton plant's DNA.

e Candidate A's answer is too short to gain 3 marks. He scores 1 mark for the idea of cutting the gene from the bacteria; the rest is too vague. Candidate B scores all 3 marks for a full answer.

Candidate A

(f) (v) Pest-resistant crops can be developed and these might get into weeds.

OCR*(Salters)* Unit 2849

Candidate B
(f) (v) Advantage: plants can be used to make useful chemicals (as here).
Disadvantage: the plants might evolve so that nothing can kill them and then take over large amounts of field space.

🖉 Candidate A is again vague. First, he does not define clearly which is an advantage and which is a disadvantage. At AS you might expect to have lines labelled 'Advantage' and 'Disadvantage', but you will not always get this at A2! However, Candidate A's first comment can be taken as an advantage and scores 1 mark. His second point does not make sense. Presumably, he meant 'these pest-resisting genes might get into weeds which would then be difficult to get rid of'. Be sure to say clearly what you mean! Candidate B has made some different, but valid, points and scores 2 marks.

Question 4

Preventing steel boats from rusting

Many steel boats have blocks of zinc fixed to their hulls to prevent them rusting. The blocks corrode rather than the iron.

Some relevant standard electrode potentials are:

	Half-equations	$E^{\ominus}/V$
A	$Zn^{2+}(aq) + 2e^- \longrightarrow Zn(s)$	−0.76
B	$Fe^{2+}(aq) + 2e^- \longrightarrow Fe(s)$	−0.44
C	$Sn^{2+}(aq) + 2e^- \longrightarrow Sn(s)$	−0.14
D	$2H^+(aq) + 2e^- \longrightarrow H_2(g)$	0 (by definition)
E	$O_2(g) + 2H_2O(l) + 4e^- \longrightarrow 4OH^-(aq)$	+0.40

(a) Draw a labelled diagram of the apparatus you would use to measure the standard electrode potential of half-equation A. *(space)* (6 marks)

(b) The two half-equations involved in rusting are B and E.
  (i) Explain how these two electrode potentials and their position in the table show that iron will react with oxygen and water. *(3 lines)* (3 marks)
  (ii) Write the equation for the reaction that occurs in part (i). *(space)* (2 marks)
  (iii) Calculate the value of $E^{\ominus}_{cell}$ for this reaction. *(space)* (2 marks)

(c) The diagram below shows a zinc block fixed to a steel hull immersed in seawater.

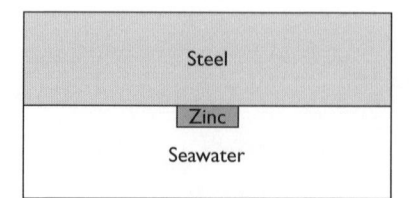

```
┌─────────────────────────┐
│         Steel           │
│        ┌─────┐          │
│        │Zinc │          │
│        └─────┘          │
│       Seawater          │
└─────────────────────────┘
```

Consider what is happening using the electrode potentials above.
  (i) Mark the flow of electrons on the diagram. (1 mark)
  (ii) Suggest why this inhibits the rusting of the iron. *(3 lines)* (2 marks)

Total: 16 marks

OCR (Salters) Unit 2849

Candidates' answers to Question 4

Candidate A
(a)

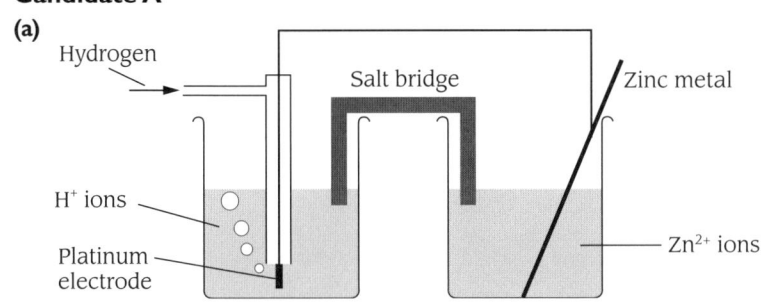

[Diagram: Left beaker labelled with Hydrogen inlet, H⁺ ions, Platinum electrode; connected via Salt bridge to right beaker with Zinc metal and Zn²⁺ ions]

Candidate B
(a)

[Diagram: Left beaker with Hydrogen at 1 atm pressure, Platinum electrode; High-resistance voltmeter (V) connected across; Salt bridge* between beakers; Right beaker with Zinc metal and Zn²⁺ ions 1.0 mol dm⁻³]

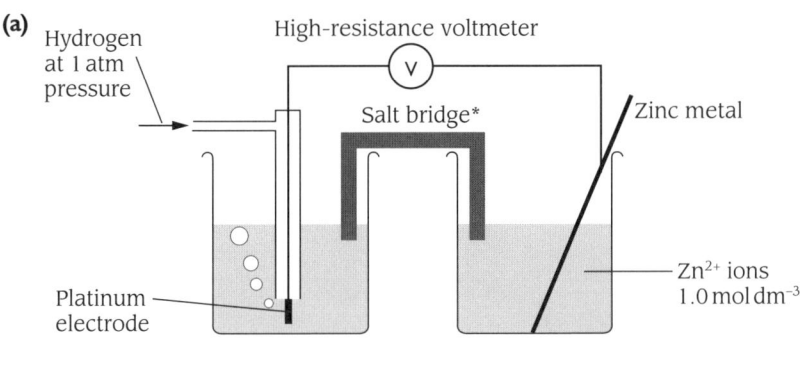

*Filter paper plus saturated potassium nitrate solution

Temperature: 298K

e Neither candidate scores full marks. Candidate A has left out the voltmeter (worth 1 mark) and all the standard conditions (worth 2 marks). She scores 3 out of 6 marks. Candidate B has not labelled the contents of the left-hand beaker and scores 5 marks.

Candidate A
(b) (i) Since B is above E, it will go backwards and make E go forwards.

Candidate B
(b) (i) Since B is the more positive electrode system, it will supply electrons through the external circuit to E. Therefore, the reaction in B will be reversed to supply electrons, and the reaction in E will go as printed.

e Candidate A's explanation is not complete. However, she has made the point about reaction B being reversed and E going in the right direction, and scores 1 mark. Candidate B has done much better. The crucial part of the argument is that *electrons flow from the more positive electrode (in this case the iron) to the more negative one, through the external circuit*. He has included this and clearly stated which is the more positive electrode. He scores all 3 marks.

Candidate A
(b) (ii) Fe(s) + O$_2$(g) + 2H$_2$O(l) ⟶ 4OH$^-$(aq) + Fe^{2+}(aq)

Candidate B
(b) (ii) 2Fe + O$_2$ + 2H$_2$O ⟶ 4OH$^-$ + 2Fe^{2+}

> *e* Candidate A has the correct idea but has not balanced the equation. She scores 1 out of 2 marks. Candidate B scores both marks. He has left out the state symbols, but they were not asked for here.

Candidate A
(b) (iii) $E^\ominus_{cell}$ = 0.40 − 0.44 = −0.04V

Candidate B
(b) (iii) $E^\ominus_{cell}$ = 0.40 − (−0.44) = +0.84

> *e* Candidate A has failed to realise that the electrode potentials are on either side of zero; thus their difference is 0.84, not 0.04. However, she gains 1 mark for using the correct units. Candidate B has the correct value for $E^\ominus_{cell}$, for 1 mark, but has failed to give units, and so loses the second mark.

Candidate A
(c) (i)

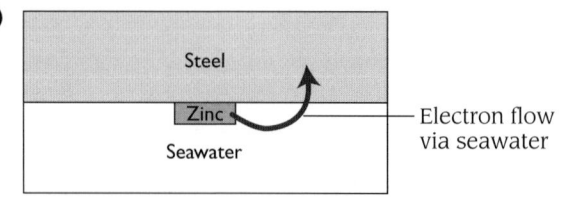

[Diagram: Steel layer above Zinc, on Seawater; arrow shows electron flow curving from Zinc through seawater to Steel — labelled "Electron flow via seawater"]

Candidate B
(c) (i)

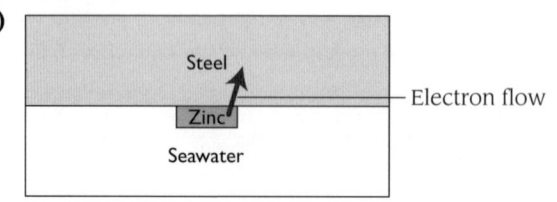

[Diagram: Steel layer above Zinc, on Seawater; arrow shows electron flow from Zinc up to Steel — labelled "Electron flow"]

> *e* Candidate B is correct, for 1 mark. Electrons only flow through metals; they never flow through solutions (ions move through solutions). Candidate A does not score.

Candidate A
(c) (ii) This inhibits rusting because the iron wants to lose electrons and in this situation they flow towards it.

Candidate B
(c) (ii) Electrons are forced onto the iron by the zinc, which corrodes instead.

> *e* Candidate A has given a good answer, for 1 mark, but it is not quite enough for full marks. The idea of zinc corroding is needed for the second mark. Candidate B scores both marks.

Question 5

Liniment

Liniment, used by athletes to relieve muscle strain, often contains 'oil of wintergreen', methyl salicylate.

(a) Identify the functional groups in methyl salicylate, which are labelled A and B. *(2 lines)* (1 mark)
(b) Describe a test and its result that would identify functional group B. *(3 lines)* (2 marks)

A chemist has available the following compounds:

(c) (i) Name compounds C and F. *(2 lines)* (2 marks)
   (ii) Name the –COCl functional group in compound D. *(1 line)* (1 mark)
   (iii) Which *two* of these compounds could the chemist react together to make methyl salicylate? *(1 line)* (2 marks)
   (iv) Draw the structure of the compound formed by reacting compound D with compound G. *(space)* (2 marks)
   (v) Place compounds C, E and G in order of *increasing* acidity, indicating the chemical theory behind your choice. *(5 lines)* (5 marks)
(d) Another chemist boiled some methyl salicylate under reflux with moderately concentrated hydrochloric acid.
   (i) Draw a labelled diagram to show how you would heat the mixture under reflux. *(space)* (3 marks)

question 5

(ii) Describe how thin-layer chromatography could be used to discover whether any starting compound remained at the end of the refluxing period. *(space + 4 lines)* (4 marks)

(iii) The products of the reaction are separated. One has an M_r of 138. Draw the structure of this compound and give the spectroscopic technique that would be used to determine the M_r. *(space, line)* (3 marks)

(iv) One of the products gives the infrared spectrum shown below. Identify this product, giving your reasons. *(5 lines)* (3 marks)

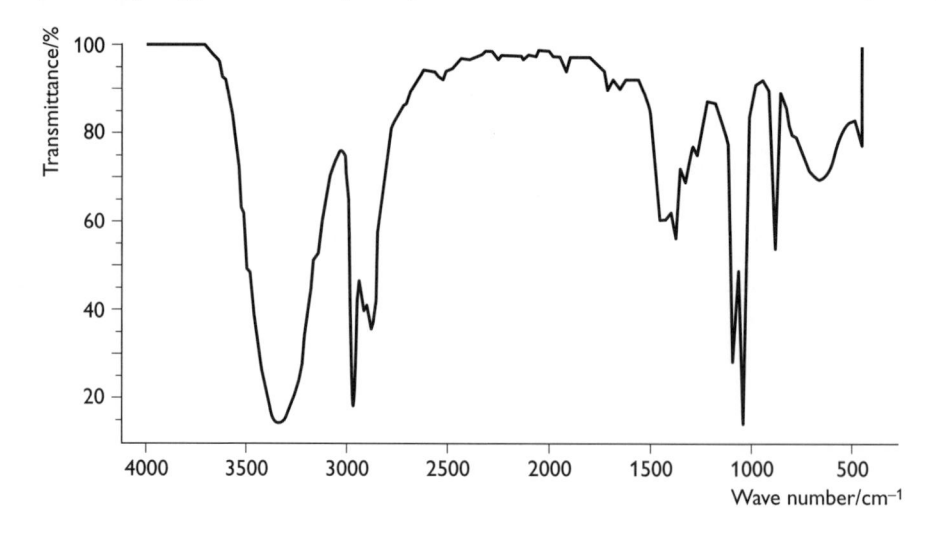

(e) If methyl salicylate had recently been discovered and basically safety-tested, name *two* sensitive groups of people on whom it would be finally tested. *(3 lines)* (2 marks)

(f) Many medicines can be improved by modifying their structures. Suggest *one* possible modification that could be made to methyl salicylate. *(3 lines)* (1 mark)

Total: 31 marks

Candidates' answers to Question 5

Candidate A
(a) A is a methyl ester; B is an alcohol

Candidate B
(a) A is an ester; B is a phenol

> Both candidates score the mark for group A, though 'ester' is quite sufficient. Only Candidate B scores the mark for group B as a hydroxyl group attached to a benzene ring is called a phenol, not an alcohol.

Candidate A
(b) Slightly acidic in solution.

Candidate B
(b) Reacts with neutral iron(III) chloride to give a purple colour.

e Candidate A scores 1 mark out of the 2. He has not said how to carry out the test. Candidate B has given the best test for a phenol and she has described it fully, so she scores 2 marks.

Candidate A
(c) (i) C is ethanoic acid; F is ethyl methanoate

Candidate B
(c) (i) C is ethanoic acid; F is methyl ethanoate

e Both candidates have identified compound C correctly and score 1 mark. Candidate B has also identified compound F correctly and scores another mark.

Candidate A has confused the parts of the ester. The $CH_3-\overset{\overset{O}{\|}}{C}-$ group comes from ethanoic acid and the OCH_3 comes from methanol — hence methyl ethanoate.

Candidate A
(c) (ii) Ethanoyl chloride

Candidate B
(c) (ii) Acyl chloride

e Candidate A has named a particular acyl choride, CH_3COCl, and so does not score the mark. Candidate B is correct, for 1 mark.

Candidate A
(c) (iii) Compounds F and G

Candidate B
(c) (iii) Compounds D and E

e Candidate B is correct and scores 2 marks. To make methyl salicylate, the acyl chloride group in D reacts with the alcohol E to form an ester. Candidate A scores nothing as he has simply selected two likely looking molecules without considering the chemical reaction.

Candidate A
(c) (iv)

question 5

Candidate B
(c) (iv)

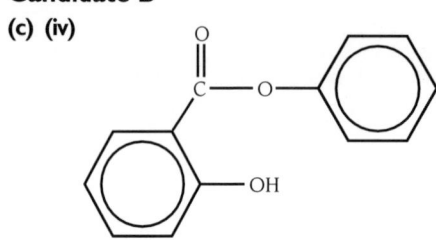

[Structure showing benzene ring with C(=O)-O- linked to another benzene ring, and OH group on the first ring]

e Candidate A scores 1 mark for identifying the correct place at which the reaction occurs. However, he has not shown an ester being formed. Candidate B has done this and scores 2 marks.

Candidate A
(c) (v) E, G, C. Alcohols are hardly acidic at all, phenols are slightly acidic and acids are acidic!

Candidate B
(c) (v) E has the lowest pH, then G, then C. This is because the anions formed by loss of a proton become more stable as one goes from alcohol to phenol to carboxylic acid.

e Candidate A has the order right and scores 2 marks for this. Then he states some correct chemistry but fails to answer the question! He has not described the chemical theory for his statement, so he does not score any further marks. Candidate B has fallen into a common trap — the lowest pH is the most acidic, not the least! She probably meant to give the same answer as Candidate A but, by (unnecessarily) mentioning pH, she has confused herself and scores zero so far. Her answer to the chemical theory part shows what she meant to say. She scores 1 mark for this but loses the final 2 marks for not mentioning that this is caused by the 'delocalisation' of the electrons and describing this in some way.

Candidate A
(d) (i)

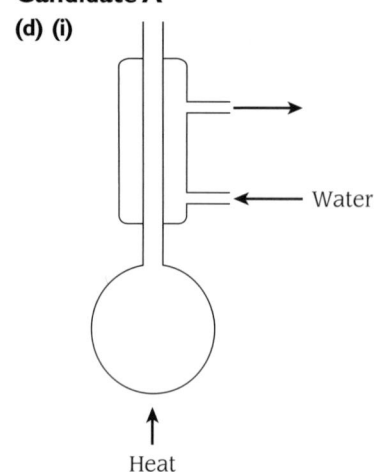

[Diagram of apparatus: flask with condenser, water inlet arrow, heat arrow below]
Water
Heat

Candidate B
(d) (i)

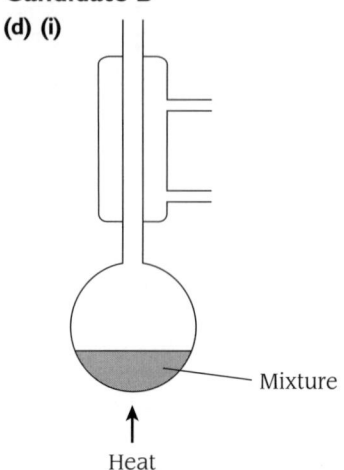

[Diagram of apparatus: flask with condenser containing mixture, heat arrow below]
Mixture
Heat

OCR (Salters) Unit 2849

☻ Neither candidate scores full marks. Candidate A does not score the mark for the flask because he has not labelled the reacting mixture. Candidate B does not score the mark for showing the water connections. Thus both score 2 marks out of 3.

Candidate A
(d) (ii) Spot, onto a thin layer plate, some mixture after reflux and some methyl salicylate. Run a chromatogram. If a dot appears at the same height as the methyl salicylate dot, this means that some remains.

Candidate B
(d) (ii) Set up the apparatus as shown in the diagram.

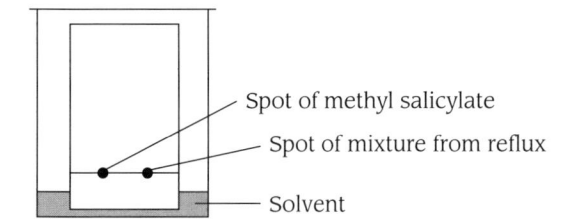

[Diagram showing TLC plate in beaker with: Spot of methyl salicylate, Spot of mixture from reflux, Solvent]

The solvent is allowed to rise up the plate. The plate is then dried and viewed under UV light. If a spot is seen above the reflux mixture that is on a level with the methyl salicylate spot, then some unreacted compound remains.

☻ Candidate A has not followed the advice in the Content Guidance to draw a diagram! Thus, he has missed out on some fairly easy marks for the method, such as having the solvent level below the spots and covering the beaker. He has also failed to say how the spots would be located. However, he scores 2 marks for the correct spots and the correct interpretation. Candidate B has given a full answer (with a diagram, which makes some of the points she has not described in writing). She scores all 4 marks.

Candidate A
(d) (iii) RMM of methyl salicylate is 154. Loss of 16 gives 138, so this must be an oxygen atom.

[Structural diagram of methyl salicylate: benzene ring with C(=O)—O—CH₃ group]

Mass spectrometry is used.

Candidate B
(d) (iii) Methyl salicylate is hydrolysed to salicylic acid and methanol. The M_r of methanol is much smaller than 138, so the compound must be salicylic acid.

question 5

A2 Chemistry

[Structure: benzene ring with -C(=O)-OH and -OH substituents]

Identified from its mass spectrum.

e Candidate A has gone off on the wrong track. He has miscalculated the M_r of methyl salicylate. (It is 152; could this be due to a misunderstanding of the number of hydrogen atoms in the substituted benzene ring — four not six?) Also, he has looked for fragments from mass spectrometry, which the question does not want. He does not score any marks for this part but he scores 1 for naming mass spectrometry as the technique. Candidate B has given the correct answer, though she is a bit cavalier in her reasoning — it would have been safer to check that the M_r of salicylic acid is 138! She scores all 3 marks.

Candidate A
(d) (iv) This compound has O–H groups (3400 cm^{-1}) and C–H groups (2900 cm^{-1}). Thus it could be either an alcohol or an acid.

Candidate B
(d) (iv) The compound has O–H groups but no C=O groups. Thus it is methanol.

e Candidate A scores 2 marks for identifying two bonds present. However, he does not score anything for the deduction. The compound could not be an acid because of the lack of C=O. Candidate B scores the 2 marks for the functional groups, though it would be safer to give the values of the absorbancies. She also goes on to identify the compound correctly from her understanding of the hydrolysis of esters, thus scoring the third mark too.

Candidate A
(e) Pregnant women and children

Candidate B
(e) The elderly and those with sensitive skins

e There are many possible answers here. Both candidates score 2 marks for sensible suggestions. Avoid giving two categories that are similar. For example, 'those with sensitive skins and those with allergies' might be deemed too similar to score 2 marks.

Candidate A
(f) Put another group on the benzene ring.

OCR (Salters) Unit 2849

Candidate B

(f) Try making the ethyl ester.

🖉 Once again there are several possibilities. Candidate B has tried to be as 'chemical' as possible and would certainly score. Candidate A also scores for a sensible suggestion that displays adequate chemical knowledge for this stage of his course.